Do I Look Like an ATM?

Do I Look Like an ATM?

A Parent's Guide to Raising Financially Responsible African American Children

SABRINA LAMB

FOUNDER/CEO, WORLDOFMONEY.ORG

Lawrence Hill Books

Chicago

Copyright © 2013 by Sabrina Lamb
All rights reserved
First edition
Published by Lawrence Hill Books, an imprint of
Chicago Review Press, Incorporated
814 North Franklin Street
Chicago, Illinois 60610

ISBN 978-1-61374-405-5

Cover design: John Yates at Stealworks.com
Cover photograph: © Ocean / Corbis
Interior design: PerfecType, Nashville, TN

Excerpt ("Our deepest fear . . . liberates others.") from *A Return to Love* by
Marianne Williamson, pages 190–91. Copyright © 1992 by Marianne Williamson. Reprinted by permission of HarperCollins Publishers.

Library of Congress Cataloging-in-Publication Data
Lamb, Sabrina.
  Do I look like an ATM? : a parents' guide to raising financially responsible
African American children / Sabrina Lamb. — 1st ed.
    p. cm.
  Includes index.
  ISBN 978-1-61374-405-5 (pbk.)
  1. African American children—Finance, Personal. 2. Children—United
States—Finance, Personal. 3. Child rearing—United States. I. Title.
  HQ784.S4L36 2013
  332.0240083'0973—dc23
                              2012040564

Printed in the United States of America
5 4 3 2 1

When you teach your son, you teach your son's son.

—TALMUD

CONTENTS

INTRODUCTION

Wake-Up Call

"You will always be your child's favorite toy." —VICKI LANSKY

CHILDREN AND MONEY are both like iron rings we put through our noses. They lead us around wherever they want. We forget that we are the ones who designed them. Simply put, your angelic darling of a child has you bamboozled. Despite your protests to the contrary, your little bundle of joy has you wrapped around her little manipulative finger because she knows you so well.

You see, from the day you placed her in her bassinette, your child has seen you coo and fawn over her so often that she can anticipate your next move, especially when it comes to money. Your unsympathetic child watches as your heart palpitates, your palms become sweaty, and your voice climbs an octave. Your perfect child is deaf to the "Do I look like an ATM?" tirades that come in response to their urgent, countless pleas to install a swimming pool in the backyard or to have a sweet sixteen party at the Waldorf Astoria.

Dear parent, you may hate to admit it, but your child was born a professional beggar. Sound a tad harsh? What about "crumb snatcher"? "Master manipulator"? How about "financial terrorist"? No need to become protective of the cute little pickpocket you are living with;

1

sooner or later, you are going to be living in the poorhouse as your firstborn robs your 401(k) retirement account to fund his wish list for countless Christmas Futures.

Remember when your child uttered his first words? Remember how you phoned your relatives, thinking your child was expressing affection for you? It was a con game. Your baby knew that, in order to get your attention to appease his fleeting desires, he would have to address you as Mama or Dada. Sadly, your child is naturally more inclined to utter "Gimme" or "I wanna" as his very first words. From his perspective, these words get right to the point without wasting time with unnecessary salutations.

Still, you may protest, "But I teach my child how to be appreciative. Really, I do!" King or Queen of Denial, far be it for me to disagree. But let's take a moment to review a scenario I'd venture to guess you've experienced a few times before:

"Can I have a dollar?" your child asks.

"Say 'please,'" you sternly reply.

"Pleeeeease," your child parrots.

Confident that in that moment you have socialized your child to become the next Mahatma Gandhi, you satisfy your child's demand. And your child believes, in spite of your denial, that you are indeed an automatic teller machine.

And so it continues.

"Open your mouth and ask for what you want," you encourage your toddler when she points to all things shiny, dangling, or easily shattered into little pieces.

And so it continues.

"Spouse of mine," you say, "little Anthony said 'please.' Isn't that soooooo precious? Now would you get that quarter away from him before he chokes himself to death?"

And so it continues.

"What did you do with the allowance I gave you yesterday? Hand me my purse. You know you need to learn how to budget!"

And so it continues.

"Honey, would you take that child to the mall and buy him another pair of Nike Air Force 1 High sneakers so he can stop all that incessant pouting?"

And so it continues.

Wouldn't you love to have a dollar for every time your child has said, "I want some money," or "Would you buy me a new toy rocket ship?" By now, you would have a fortune sufficient to retire and cruise around the world on your private yacht. But your wonderful teenager has other plans. These scenarios occur in countless households all over America and all over the world. Parents like you have been duped into spending their lives being manipulated by sweet little beggars. What else would one call a human being who spends the majority of her life uttering (even in her sleep), "Can I have _____?"

It did not start off that way. When you decided to have a child, you thought that you were in control. More than anything in the world, you desired to bestow limitless love on your child, perhaps even more than you had personally experienced. You were determined to be your definition of a perfect parent. And you were sure your child would bond with you and love you in return. Your worth as a parent and as a human being would be reflected in the love of your child, who would boast, "I have the best mommy and daddy in the whole world."

That was the starting plan, but that is not the way it turned out. When it comes to financial matters, your child has learned that he can manipulate you because you are so concerned with how he feels about you. And as long as his loving you is more important to you than your nurturing a compassionate, financially responsible, self-reliant, service-minded child who will serve the world, you can forget about sailing around the world on your private yacht. Avoiding (or refusing) opportunities to teach children about money and to take loving care of yourself will result in your children becoming manipulative and selfish adults who lack the tools to survive and prosper in the world.

But not to worry—there is hope, and you are not alone. *Do I Look Like an ATM? A Parent's Guide to Raising Financially Responsible African American Children* is here to the rescue.

As the founding chief executive officer of the financial education organization WorldofMoney.org, I am uniquely qualified to write this book because of my blunt conversations with and candid observations of children like yours. And while I adore children and believe that it is my life mission to empower them through financial education, my compassion for them does not extend to allowing them to marinate in the illusion of entitlement and ignorance.

And, after reading this book, nor will you, dear parent.

Children came into the world without a reflection button that would enable them to say, "Oh, mother and father of mine, there is no need to waste your hard-earned dollars on a new PlayStation. That would be frivolous. May we please sit down as a family and review our household expenses? May we review where we can eliminate unnecessary expenditures? May we designate each Friday to be Coupon Clipping Night?" Unless you gave birth to frugal billionaire Warren Buffet, you'll never hear your son say, "Mother dear, why not purchase my school clothes when they are on sale? Our family could financially benefit from the savings, and then we could donate the clothes that I have outgrown to charity."

Children, being the brilliant beings from heaven that they are, know that while they are tugging on your heartstrings, they are nibbling away at your common sense—all the while draining your savings account. Children also recognize when their shell game is in grave danger of coming to a screeching halt.

Children are keenly aware of adults who are not enamored of their emotional manipulation. I still remember one such saucer-eyed, twelve-year-old girl. She nervously shifted next to her mother as I challenged the parents in the room to teach their children to become financial team leaders in their families. A look of terror clouded her face when her mother told her, "You are going to the World of Money Youth Financial Education Institute this summer. Since you don't want to listen to me, maybe if you hear it from somebody else you'll appreciate the fact that my money does not grow on trees!"

Along with her mother's admonition, the young girl had heard my keynote speech, during which I demanded that the children tell me whom they thought was responsible for their financial future. I required many of them to calculate how much money they had coerced from their parents in the form of Christmas and birthday gifts. Many could not even recall what they had received for Christmas just four months earlier. They looked as if their hands had just been caught in the proverbial cookie jar.

Other young people were apathetic or defiant, saying that they were not interested in learning about personal finance. "I'm bored!" a young man of sixteen said, shrugging his shoulders. Another girl, age eighteen, shared that learning about money was a complete waste of her time. After all, she said, "My mother got me. College and whatever else. She's going to keep paying for what I want." In response, her mother looked as if she wanted to slide under her chair from sheer embarrassment.

To all these young people, I said, "Before you are issued a driver's license, an adult teaches you how to drive. Accordingly, until you know how to manage money, stop begging to spend money you did not earn, including your parents'. Whether you learn how to grow and manage money is really no one's responsibility but your own. So continue being bored, young man, so that high-interest credit card companies can market to you and by the age of twenty-one you'll have a credit report that looks like the target at a shooting range. Continue, young lady, expecting your mother to take care of you financially. And what will you have when it comes time to take care of your mother in her retirement years?"

Silence.

Three months later, this eighteen-year-old, whose mother enrolled her at the WorldofMoney.org Youth Financial Education Institute, had undergone a life-changing transformation. She earned a perfect score on the final exam and graduated at the top of a class of her peers. Her mother witnessed a dramatic change in her child: "Now she begs me to open a mutual fund account for her, and I don't remember the last time she went on a shopping spree. My daughter really wants to help lower our household expenses. She has become a financial team leader in our family." The principles that guided this mother's child at the institute permeate each chapter in this book.

Do I Look Like an ATM? is not another personal finance book designed to educate you on budgeting and hot stock tips that will make you and your children millionaires overnight. This is not another personal finance book intended to advise you on disciplined saving and investing. You may already have read many books written by popular financial gurus who appear often in the media and dazzle you with their expertise. However, financial experts, blogs, and television segments have not inspired you to have a *moneylogue* with your child. This book encourages parents to take an emotional inventory of toxic, unconscious spending as well as discuss our society's tendency to greed and hoard—and transfer those behaviors on to our children.

You might be saying, "I'll start after I improve my knowledge." Or "I'll get to it when my tax refund arrives. Then we'll have some money to talk about." Or "Next year, I'll start off on a brand-new foot." Or "I've made a complete mess of my financial life—I don't know where to start with my child. I don't like looking as if I am out of control." You have not been able to move forward because you have quietly repeated these mantras. You are frozen with fear, comforted by inaction, and confused about to how to change your family's financial culture. You hope that your children and grandchildren do not repeat your blind mistakes—the ones you have made simply because you were never taught otherwise. Yet until now, you have not taken affirmative action to empower your family's financial legacy.

Perhaps as a child, the only parental figure you observed saving money was an elderly relative who kept her money nestled under her mattress or between the pages of the Bible she kept on her nightstand. Or maybe you remember those affluent kids at school who were members of the economics club, whose nannies drove the newest foreign-made automobiles to pick them up from school. You may have already heard about the Dow Jones Industrial Average or listened to heated debates about the economic stability of world markets during the last two minutes of your television news broadcast. Your eyes may glaze over at the mention of commodities, and you may think that they are viruses you contract as a side effect of the flu vaccine.

Do I Look Like an ATM? is meant to inspire and direct you toward using your children as a catalyst to hit the reset button, not only in your financial life but in that of your family. It is my hope that *Do I Look Like an ATM?* will eradicate your family's toxic financial culture so that you can empower the next generation by raising your children to be financially responsible adults, even if you were never given a comprehensive financial education.

Perhaps you're a parent who dreads taking a close inventory of your relationship with money. Secretly, you want your children to have access to far more financial education than you ever dreamed of. You know that your children need it. You have observed your children's obsession with money: they love spending yours. You are unnerved by the media influences that inform your family's financial decisions.

Or perhaps you have noticed that your child prefers to save her earnings and her financial gifts but is tightfisted when it comes to sharing. You may have a child who is displaying the names of six different high-profile designers on his body at any given time. You may complain to your friends or scold your children about their disrespect for money, yet because your own relationship with money is fragile, the conversation rarely moves from emotional disapproval to an educated, interactive discussion.

This book can change that.

You will read personal experiences from other parents throughout this holistic guide, which is designed to help you and your child work from the same financial page without ego and without shame. This new relationship with your children will be less likely to be fraught with stress concerning money. And you will feel less frustrated by how you and your child communicate.

In reality, your children are on your side. Your children may not know or admit it, because they believe their mission in life is to make you believe that anything you find relevant is not worthy of their attention. In their minds, whatever issues are relevant to parents could not ever reach the cool factor. However, because children do not understand the full impact that money has on their lives, your children often use money as unconsciously as we all have. Over the years, I have observed that discussing money matters is taboo in many families, akin to talking about sex or politics. But having these conversations is actually one of the best investments you can make in your relationship with your child.

Do I Look Like an ATM? will support you in raising financially responsible adults, one child at a time, but it will also help you achieve financial and emotional harmony in your family. This book will provide the language and tactical strategies needed to successfully communicate with your children. It will also help you explore emotions that may have blocked you from attempting to take your first step forward. This book will teach you how to discuss the subject of money in a meaningful manner and engage your children in making smart financial decisions.

IN 2005 WHEN I established the WorldofMoney.org Youth Financial Education Institute, I had no plans to write a book. Then I heard from parents from around the United States and around the world—from Kenya to Australia. They got in touch with me to ask for advice on how to nurture financially responsible children when they themselves were devoid of this knowledge.

Each year, parents who attended orientations for the institute would pose questions on every possible subject: "My child has no interest in learning about money. How do I change that?" "Should I give my child an allowance?" "How do I release the shame of messing up my own finances?" "My grown son won't contribute to the household. How do I change that?" "My daughter refuses to wear discounted clothing. What must I do?"

Children had their concerns too. One young boy shared, "My mother took my money out of my piggy bank without telling me." One girl said, "My mother uses my money but won't give it back to me." Still another young man said, "My dad gives me money because he won't come to my basketball games. I take it, but I'm still mad at him." A hush would spread through the auditorium when these young voices shared their emotions and anger regarding how they had observed their own parents relate to money. These young people would speak up even with their parents sitting only a few rows away. Trickles of perspiration would sneak down the side of my face as I racked my brain to come up with answers that would not further embarrass the parents in question but, at the same time, would address the children's concerns.

During my private conversations with parents and children, I encouraged them to seize these moments to hit the reset button in their relationships with money.

Nailah's Story

Nailah, age thirteen, shared: "Before I went to World of Money, I didn't know about the stock market, stocks, bonds, or loans. Matter of fact, I did not really care. I didn't know about the bills my parents had to pay. All I cared was that there was a roof over my head, clothes on my back, and food on the table. Basically, I was living an unstable life, without foundation, and not even knowing it. Now that I have experienced World of Money, I pay for a lot of my own things; I am more knowledgeable about my financial environment and future. I started my own mutual fund account. I have my own job, and I have my own business where I use my creative abilities to draw, paint, and sculpt and then sell my artwork to interested people."

Quran's Story

"The World of Money Youth Financial Education Institute made me think about my future and what I want to become," Quran said. "Without your confidence I would still be spending money on what I wanted rather than spending it on what I need. I have stopped asking for what I want and started saying, 'How can I earn?' World of Money taught me things that nobody else would, besides my mom, such as finance, banking, money, and building a financially stable future for myself and my family."

Ciana's Story

Ciana agrees. "Thanks to learning about the world of money, I'm smarter about money, and I have learned how to grow our money—like the concept of compound interest. I will know when people are trying to take my money, and most importantly I will know how to increase my wealth and stay financially safe. I think money is very important in our society, and I am glad that I have learned to earn, save, invest, and donate my money wisely.

"Now that I have been introduced to the world of money, I have the keys that will open the doors to making my dreams come true. I will start making smart money decisions now to ensure my future prosperity. I will go to the college of my choosing. I will not be held back by the people who don't know what they are doing with their lives. During World of Money, I learned many things that will help me now and in the future. I learned about investments, stocks, bonds, insurance, and how to change my future dreams into future plans. Volunteers took time out of their busy schedules to teach me and my peers how to make money work for us and how to be the ones doing the hiring. I now know the dangers of credit cards and about how important it is to have a good FICO score. All the tricks of Rent-A-Center, payday loans, e-mail scams, phone scams, and many more have been brought to my attention so that I don't fall into debt. I realized that my future is not that far away and that the path to financial success starts right now."

Our children are waiting to learn how to harness this powerful currency. Applying the concepts in *Do I Look Like an ATM?* will help you provide an ethically sound foundation. This book is the first stepping-stone on that path to financial harmony within your family.

1

Assessing the Situation

"Children have never been good at listening to their elders, but they have never failed to imitate them." —JAMES BALDWIN

YOUR CHILD IS already aware of the quality of your money management skills. He may not know the balance in your savings account or if you have been investing in a mutual fund, but your child is very intuitive. Since his birth, your child has observed your emotions about money and your relationship to it. Money had his attention as soon as the little cupcake figured out what it could do, and ever since money and its power have captured his imagination.

Parents owe their children the opportunity to be financially literate and self-reliant at a very early age. This trait is especially important given the fact that there will be roller-coaster economic cycles. Those who will be most stable are the individuals who learn very early on how to earn, manage their finances, and examine their money personalities.

■ What Is My Child's Money Personality?

	YES	NO
1. My child only wears designer clothing and shoes.	_____	_____
2. My child gives his/her money away to friends.	_____	_____
3. My child saves every penny he/she earns.	_____	_____
4. My child has stolen money.	_____	_____
5. My child does not remember what gifts he/she received last Christmas.	_____	_____
6. My child becomes angry if he/she is refused money.	_____	_____
7. My child receives an allowance.	_____	_____
8. My child has his/her own business.	_____	_____
9. My child is curious about investing.	_____	_____
10. My child's first words were "Gimme gimme."	_____	_____
11. My child loves to make bank deposits.	_____	_____
12. My child has asked, "How may I earn?" or "Can I get a job?"	_____	_____
13. My child has been deceptive about a money issue.	_____	_____
14. If my child has money of his/her own, he/she is reluctant to spend it.	_____	_____
15. My child is eager to collect monies or goods to help the needy.	_____	_____
16. My child believes money is a tool of the devil.	_____	_____

■ What Is My Child's Money Personality? Scoring Guide

First, know that no matter what result you calculate, that score does not mean your child possesses entrenched values. With your guidance, influence, and financial education, your child's relationship can be channeled in the direction that will benefit his or her future.

Your totals point toward those traits that your child may have developed under your nose or as a result of *your* influence. The quiz will also reveal which of your child's money traits may need nurturing.

Of course, as a parent, you hope that your child has the personality of a saver and philanthropist. But those characteristics must be nurtured to ward off the selfish, impulsive, spendthrift tendencies of most children.

Answer Points

1. Yes = 1, No = 2
2. Yes = 1, No = 2
3. Yes = 2, No = 1
4. Yes = 1, No = 2
5. Yes = 2, No = 1
6. Yes = 1, No = 2
7. Yes = 2, No = 1
8. Yes = 3, No = 1
9. Yes = 3, No = 1
10. Yes = 1, No = 2
11. Yes = 3, No = 1
12. Yes = 3, No = 1
13. Yes = 1, No = 2
14. Yes = 1, No = 2
15. Yes = 3, No = 1
16. Yes = 1, No = 3

32–38: Excellent

Your child is demonstrating the traits of a millionaire mindset. Congratulations! With careful nurturing and financial education, continue to encourage your child to build toward a financially secure life.

26–31: Good

While your child is off to a good start, she could be encouraged to take on added money management responsibilities and to learn more along with you.

20–25: Fair

Your child's perceptions and behaviors are too close to the danger zone for comfort. Any major event or influence could sway him toward ignoring the power of money or becoming entrenched in greed.

16–19: Toxic

Without immediate analysis and behavior modification, your child's attitudes or outside influences could negatively impact the quality of her life and that of your family's financial culture.

Akil's Story

In 2006, eighteen-year-old Akil, a student at the WorldofMoney.org Youth Financial Education Institute, said angrily, "I'm getting ready to go out on my own, and nobody ever taught me anything about money. Until now, I didn't know anything about this stuff."

Jeff Gardere, PhD, coauthor of *Practical Parenting*, believes, "Though it sounds emotionally heavy, parents do owe it to their children to teach them how to be financially literate and responsible at a very early age. This is especially important given the fact that there are going to be challenging financial times for the foreseeable future. Both parents and children need to build a financially secure foundation. And in spite of what the media reports about our economic health as a nation, families can still prosper if they take corrective action to do so."

In "Boosting Financial Literacy in America: A Role for State Colleges and Universities" (*Perspectives*, American Association of State Colleges and Universities, Fall 2010), Thomas Harnisch discusses the urgent reasons your children must be taught personal finance. Harnisch writes, "Low levels of financial literacy may lead to poor health, decreased quality of life, and lower college attainment levels. Plus, the cost of poor financial decision-making and planning often gets shifted to the community, state, and nation through higher prices for financial products, and greater use of public 'safety net' programs."

A lack of basic understanding of the world of money can lead to emotional stress, depression, apathy, and dependent behavior. And when these things become entrenched in one's family and children over a generation, the results are debilitating, creating aimless, frustrated young adults. If children do not have a clear sense of the importance of the world of money and if the basics are only brought to their attention during a crisis, they will not know how to respond to and navigate life's economic roller coasters.

Laura Levine, executive director of Jump$tart Coalition for Personal Financial Literacy, noted, "The lack of financial knowledge and ability among America's youth is also a serious problem that is not going to improve on its own. Additional emphasis needs to be placed on teaching personal finance concepts in schools, to prepare young people for their lives as independent consumers rather than waiting to offer remedial financial education after they have begun to make mistakes."

While that is true, a child's first financial instruction, whether positive or negative, occurs in the home. Parents and youth cannot wait for the government to provide financial education. Perhaps you were never taught about the world of money. Your parents and grandparents may have unconsciously passed down negative behaviors regarding money to your generation. Some of us may feel shame, depression, and anger about our present financial status. We may spend money to feed our low self-esteem or to try to impress others who are probably more broke than we are. These disturbing tendencies are then adopted by our children. Our children begin to believe that they are valued by how much money they can spend and whose logo they wear on their bodies.

Taught frivolous spending, our children will whine and resist all notions of community service and philanthropic donation. Children will grow to believe that they should only serve their communities if they receive a measurable benefit in return. Further, our children may despise or become jealous of the financially successful, or they may camouflage their fear of money by hurling insults at those who are wealthy.

How did we ever enter into these toxic relationships with money when it's really just a tool for basic survival? Members of the black community are often characterized as poor, downtrodden, underprivileged, and disadvantaged. And while that may be true for some individuals, no community that is projected to spend $1.1 trillion annually by 2012, exceeding the gross domestic products of Spain and Canada, could ever be considered poor.[1]

Marketing Forecast also reports that the top five categories of expenditure were goods that have zero appreciative value: rental housing, food, cars, clothing, and health care. It is not being suggested that blacks are sitting on piles of cash, but what is clear is that in far too many instances, the cash available is not being used to create even a modest financial cushion.

Furthermore, without financial education, blacks are far more likely to be subject to high interest rates, high insurance costs, and expensive food from substandard supermarkets. It is often argued that the focus for fiscal responsibility must be aimed at government and Wall Street. That may be true, but while we are waiting for squabbling politicians to bridge a compromise, we as parents have the opportunity to bail ourselves out.

Starting now.

---

1. Jeff Humphreys, director of the Selig Center for Economic Growth, has reported that US black buying power is projected to top $1.1 trillion by 2012.

Sobering Statistics

Financial Education

About 41 percent of US adults, or more than 92 million people living in America, gave themselves a grade of C, D, or F on their knowledge of personal finance, suggesting there is considerable room for improvement. This feeling of failure is highest among Gen Y adults, reaching 47 percent. And 80 percent of adults agree or strongly agree that they would benefit from advice and answers to everyday financial questions from a professional (35 percent strongly agree).

Budget

Showing no improvement since 2007, less than half of adults—42 percent—keep close track of their spending. Nearly 16 million adults (7 percent) don't know how much they spend on food, housing, and entertainment, and do not monitor their overall spending.

Debt and Credit Cards

More than 58 million adults, or 26 percent, admit to not paying all of their bills on time. Among African Americans, this number is at 51 percent. In the last twelve months, 15 percent of adults, or nearly 34 million people, have been late making a credit card payment, and 8 percent (18 million people) have missed a payment entirely. More than 13 million adults (6 percent) report that their household carries credit card debt of $10,000 or more from month to month, and the same number have debts in collection, are seriously considering filing for bankruptcy, or have already done so within the past three years.

Housing

More than 94 million people, or 42 percent of adults, currently have a home mortgage, and of those, 28 percent say that the terms of their mortgage somehow turned out to be different than they expected. Either the payment amounts or terms of the loans were different than expected or the interest rates or their durations were different than expected.

Savings

One-third of adults (32 percent), or 72 million people, report that they have no savings, and only 23 percent are now saving more than they did a year ago because of the current economic climate. Nearly half (48 percent) of Gen Y adults—more than any other age group—report having no savings. Of those with no savings, more than one in four reports that, if faced with an emergency, they would charge that expense to a credit card (29 percent) or take out a loan (26 percent), thus adding to their debt load.

Spending

Fifty-seven percent of adults report spending less than they did a year ago. However, 45 percent of those now spending less admit that, if their financial situation were to improve within the next year, they would resume their previous spending habits.

Credit Score

Nearly two-thirds (64 percent), or 144 million people, have not ordered their credit reports in the past year—in spite of the fact that they are free of charge. Additionally, more than one-third (37 percent) admit that they do not know their credit scores.

Retirement

One-third of adults (33 percent), or more than 74 million people, do not put any part of their annual household income toward retirement. This is up from 28 percent in 2008.

Insurance

More than one in ten adults (13 percent) do not have medical insurance, and this number grows to 20 percent among Gen Y adults. Nearly three in four (72 percent) do not have long-term care insurance, including 65 percent of adults aged 65 and older. This is more than 24 million people.

■ The Life of a Financially Empowered Child

The issues of financial security and financial education are of paramount concern to many parents of African American children. In the wake of a tumultuous economy, parents are struggling to empower themselves but, at the same time, are at a loss regarding how to raise financially responsible children.

According to the Jump$tart Coalition for Personal Financial Literacy, African Americans' level of financial education lags behind that of whites, and the gap is steadily growing. This report is substantiated by Target Market News research of African American buying power, which topped $803 billion in 2008. Rental housing led purchases (with $166.3 billion), followed by food ($65.3 billion), cars/trucks ($31.5 billion), apparel products/services ($26.9 billion), health care ($17.9 billion), insurance ($16.6 billion), telephone services ($14.0 billion), housewares ($596 million), sports/recreation equipment ($475 million), and books ($257 million). None of the aforementioned products retain the retail cost value of the initial purchase. What these numbers reveal is that African Americans tend to wield their tremendous buying power on products with little or zero monetary value. The relative paucity of investments in savings, retirement, or investment vehicles held by blacks contributes to the growth of gaping wealth disparities.

Not only are African Americans less likely to own retirement accounts or investment securities, members of this community are far less likely to own homes, which remains the largest engine of wealth creation for most Americans. And when they do own homes, they tend to have less equity in them, in large part because they live in communities where prices appreciate more slowly. These outcomes are a result of a lack of financial education.

Money is a metaphor for the power, or lack thereof, one feels in the world. Show me an adult who abuses money, and I will show you an adult who feels vulnerable. Many African Americans possess a dysfunctional belief that their ability to spend reflects their acceptance by mainstream society. The spending habits of many African Americans reflect a deep-seated pathology, one that leads to flying through life financially blind.

The problem stems from the fact that young black people are less likely than their white counterparts to receive money management education in school *or* from their own parents. Following the behavior patterns of their parents, African American youth are more likely than their white peers to use credit and debit cards. Furthermore, black youth are least likely to have part-time or summer jobs in high school, thus depriving them of opportunities to become familiar with earning money before they reach adulthood. By that time, their white counterparts have gained a head start in practicing and learning valuable financial-literacy skills. Money management is not a predominant aspect of the African American culture; for generations, advocacy has focused more on civil rights than on "silver" rights.

African Americans, in general, perform better in the area of spending—rather than saving—when compared to any other racial group. The emphasis on consumption by African Americans is unconsciously passed down through generations and shows little signs of abating. The Selig Center for Economic Growth, which chronicles consumer buying power, points out that blacks spent a larger percentage of their income on natural gas, electricity, telephone services, and footwear, and a higher proportion of their money on groceries, housing, and women's and girls' clothing than other ethnic groups. Admittedly, food, clothing, electricity, and telephone service are necessities. But studies show that African Americans still set aside only a small portion of their incomes for a rainy day. According to a study commissioned by Prudential Financial, only 20 percent of African Americans believe that they are on track to meet their savings goals for retirement, and nearly 40 percent report that they have not begun. Even with their unconscious spending, 60 percent of African Americans surveyed have less than $50,000 in company retirement plans, and only 23 percent have more than $100,000.

2

Origins of Resistance

If your child tells you that she doesn't want to learn how to use money
positively . . . then tell her, until she does, to stop using yours.

USING HER DISTRAUGHT mother as a living ATM, seventeen-year-old Monica insists on wearing only designer clothing. When asked how her college was going to be paid for, she quipped, "I'm not worried about it. My mother got me." Her mother's professional network tried to help provide employment for Monica, but she has been fired from three positions for tardiness and insubordination. Monica believes that employers need to stop being so controlling: "It's just a job." Nathan has had a similar experience. He dropped out of high school, works part-time at a local bodega, and is paid cash off the books. He receives public assistance because of his alleged disability and at age sixteen has two children with two different teenage girls. Nathan wears diamond studs in both ears, owns an iPod and iPhone, and drives a late-model Cadillac Escalade. He lives with his aunt in a housing project.

Before I founded the WorldofMoney.org Youth Financial Education Institute, I surveyed parents for their opinions about creating an organization dedicated to the financial education of children. Frankly, I was stunned by the remarks parents offered: "Kids aren't interested in nothing like that." "Parents don't want their children to know nothing about money; they are too busy spending it to teach it." "The love of money is a sin." "Money is for rich people."

Other naysayers expressed an irrational belief that there was something wrong with children knowing too much about money, and some thought that this subject should be reserved for wealthy people, for whom some parents expressed distrust. Other responses broke down along racial lines, with some expressing the belief that those outside of the African American community were more adept in their relationships with money.

Last year, while speaking for nearly an hour with a legendary television broadcaster, I shared how empowered I believed his audience could become through a program about the urgency of financial education. This popular television host flatly refused, saying that he would rather keep his program's focus on how white people established the entire financial system and then set about to rip off African Americans. He believed that people of color had been oppressed by Wall Street and that wealthy people, by and large, were not to be trusted.

When I discussed the enormous economic power of the African American community and how all parents wanted to learn how to teach their children how to harness that power, he adamantly refused to move his audience toward a conversation about financial independence. During his thirty years on the air, this popular host refused to produce one segment or program on the urgency of financial education. This gentle giant quipped during one conversation, "We must focus solely on white people and all that they have taken for four hundred years from people of African descent. We must continue to hold them accountable." In essence, he preferred to keep his vast audience ignorant and disenfranchised on this subject. He remained determined to rest complete financial responsibility in the hands of white people. While not denying the historical atrocities experienced by black people, one must not ignore that today there are financial measures that African Americans can take to empower their families.

Fortunately, when the WorldofMoney.org Youth Financial Education Institute launched in 2005, the naysayers, like this broadcaster, were proven wrong. I know that these detractors have their own issues with money, and like birds of a feather, they prefer that everyone keep them company in their ignorance.

Many parents resist talking about financial matters because of the same charged emotions they feel in discussing sex, which primarily stem from conflicting messages they learned during their own childhoods. According to Debrena Jackson Gandy, author and international transformational consultant,

> Parents have negative associations about the issues of money because they possess conflicting core beliefs. In the black community, conflicting core beliefs could stem from church teachings, and the way the scriptures are interpreted in the Bible establishes a moral basis for our relationship with money. Many parents are taught that it is harder for a camel to get through the eye of a needle than for a rich man to get into heaven. Thus one concludes, "Well, I want to get into heaven. And a rich man can't get into heaven. So I will focus on getting into heaven, and not being rich or financially secure." Alternatively, due to their racial and ethnic influences, some parents believe that it is pious to live a life of poverty. These parents believe that to be "black" is to be "poor." Thus, they believe that they maintain their racial allegiance by struggling financially.

In this world of conflicting beliefs, the net effect can be negative because of societal and family influences that transfer feelings of guilt, shame, struggle, and lack on those in their family and environment. The quality of the words parents use to talk about money reflects their internal conflict. This conflict creates a warped sense of the value and power of money.

For many of us, anxieties originate from a state of being conflicted about establishing a financial foundation and passing earthly wealth to our children while still being true to our spiritual doctrine's view of finding our true wealth in an afterlife.

Maxine's Story

Maxine is a forty-two-year-old mother.

"Last weekend, my fifteen-year-old son, Marcus, and I had a heart-to-heart conversation, and we told each other everything. I told him about the shameful things that I have done that I've tried to forget for years, about the embarrassing things, about all of my past behaviors with regard to handling money.

"Marcus admitted that he knew quite a bit about our financial situation, but for some reason this past weekend, we both needed to come clean. I needed to share about certain parts of my past that I'm not proud of. It was really hard at first, and I wondered if I was doing the right thing, but then the wall fell down. Marcus told me about how he felt growing up and all of the things that he had done to try to forget. Was it hard? Yes. Was it embarrassing? Yes. Was it worth it? Completely.

"Now, more than ever before, my son trusts me with his deepest secrets, and that I trust him enough to ask him to be a financial team leader in our family. This only happened last night, and to be honest I wasn't sure if it was something that other parents did or not, but I had prayed about it and had asked God what to do, and I felt directed to do this.

"After my divorce, for years, Marcus blamed me for not only ending the relationship with his father, but ending the seemingly idyllic existence we had in the suburbs. While my husband was bankrupting the family with his addiction to gambling, our beautiful home in southeast Queens was in foreclosure. My husband still refuses to admit that he had hidden the mortgage bills from me. But I told Marcus that I no longer wanted to point fingers at his father and to accept my responsibility for my passive role in our family's financial affairs. Perhaps if I had, I could have stopped my mindless shopping trips, saved money, and avoided losing our home. But now I believe there is no such thing as a coincidence. Of course, I would have preferred to avoid the upheaval in my life, but now I have a financial counselor, and my son helps around the house.

"Marcus had a lot on his heart too. He hated hearing his father and I constantly fight over money. He said, 'Sometimes, I covered my ears with my iPod earphones to drown out your arguments, but even though the music was blasting, I knew the arguments were over when one or both of you left the house. The tension left then, too. After a few hours, you would come home with all these shopping bags or Dad would come home drunk and see them, and then y'all would start fighting all over again. I just never understood any of it. But if I had known that things were that bad, I would never have asked you for all that electronic stuff. I mean, I knew if I really wanted it, then you would give it to me. Dad would always say no to whatever I asked. But now that I know what I do, I'm just glad that we're together as a family. Sure, I still love Dad and see he has a lot of issues, but I don't want to be a burden.'

"When Marcus said what he had to say, we hugged. I released being the mother who was more focused on filling my closets than my son's heart. And Marcus became determined to be the young man I always wanted him to be.

"I am excited about our new relationship. I am tired of living a financial lie. Now it is time to rebuild. Many of my friends are living financial lies, and their children are the witness. I didn't want that type of relationship with my child or in my life. I wanted a relationship where I could tell him anything. I think I've finally got that, and I can't wait to see what happens next for us!"

These attitudes are in no way unique to the African American community. African American and Latino parents, as well as those from other ethnic groups, responded in droves, either by enrolling their children in the WorldofMoney.org Youth Financial Education Institute or by requesting information on how they could teach their children in their home countries. Parents throughout the United States, Australia,

Canada, United Kingdom, and Kenya responded to my television appearances, pleading for the institute to launch in their country. Their impassioned pleas demonstrated that there is an urgent global need to support parents in their quest to financially educate their children.

While some school districts and corporations encourage the notion of financial education for young people, many do little beyond creating financial teaching materials. Empowering our children through financial education begins at home with parents, because beliefs about money are formed in the home. As generational wealth slips through our fingers, it is no longer advisable for parents and children alike to remain ignorant of these issues, particularly when a parent is confronted with them daily.

The Center for American Progress[1] surveyed African Americans and Latinos and found that African American respondents were most receptive to education and counseling provided to consumers. Hispanic respondents also strongly favored consumer education campaigns, as did white respondents, albeit to a lesser extent.

Digging Deeper

- ◉ Fifty-six percent of African Americans described personal debt levels as a "serious problem" at the beginning of the Center for American Progress survey. When asked again at the end of the poll, 70 percent of African Americans described debt as a "serious problem," compared to only 56 percent of all respondents.
- ◉ African American respondents were much less likely to see household debt as a "middle-class" issue. Only 54 percent said that debt is an issue that faces middle-class families as well as low-income households, compared to 79 percent of all respondents.
- ◉ Thirty-nine percent of African American respondents thought the economy was most responsible for the debt problem, compared to only 24 percent of all respondents.

---

1. Center for American Progress poll, July 19, 2006.

❯ African American respondents were most concerned about not being able to have a secure retirement (43 percent were "very worried") and not having enough money to pay the bills (34 percent).

❯ A total of 28 percent of African American respondents reported personal debt over $20,000, including 12 percent who reported debt in excess of $40,000.

❯ Seventy-seven percent of African American respondents "strongly favored" government efforts to alleviate debt by expanding access to affordable housing, health care, and student loans. African Americans also "strongly favored" expanding consumer education (79 percent), and cracking down on abusive lending practices (76 percent).

Our children are witnesses to these statistics. Parents often lack the confidence to discuss financial matters with their children. Some avoid having these conversations with their children to spare themselves the embarrassment of not appearing "all knowing" in the eyes of their children. Many parents have shared that they feel more confident speaking with their children about puberty and politics than about money, while others give themselves a C in their ability to do so.

According to the TD Bank Financial Literacy Poll, fathers indicated more confidence than mothers in discussing these matters. And while both mothers and fathers agreed that budgeting was necessary, 42 percent of both parents had not created a budget.

Children also witness the fundamental responsibility of their parents. Though WorldofMoney.org parents wish that courses in financial education were available in their children's schools, we must not wait for the Department of Education to empower our children, especially while our children model our toxic or semitoxic behaviors and will each live to take on more than $200,000 worth of debt on average before the age of twenty-five.

As you consider the information outlines on these pages, please answer the following questions:

- ❯ What benefit will you bring to your family and to your community if you purposely encourage their ignorance about money?
- ❯ How will your family culture change if you include your child in your money discussions?
- ❯ When should your child begin building toward his or her financial future?
- ❯ Who or what are your child's biggest outside influencers with regard to money?
- ❯ What are your personal views about "financially successful" individuals?
- ❯ What is the benefit to your child of your failing to have positive financial discussions with him or her?

Many African American parents acknowledge that, financially speaking, they are aboard runaway trains. At the same time, however, they need and want to know how to raise financially responsible children so that they can avoid the mistakes their parents made. These vulnerable parents are intimidated by their own finances and are haunted by their financial pasts. Moreover, they try to balance their love for their children with their financial responsibilities, but they are paralyzed by ignorance about their own toxic personal relationships with money. Many remain at a crossroads, unclear about which direction they should take. As a parent, you need to face your own fears and discover that what you are afraid of is not such a big threat after all.

In order to take action, you may need a powerful, deeply rooted motivation. Become motivated to overcome financial obstacles so you can manage money instead of allowing money and your children to manage you. Let your motivation be the catalyst to change the financial culture in your family, not only for you but also for your descendants. A parent's duty in the area of finances is to provide her children with the keys to the world. Utilizing the action points in *Do I Look Like an ATM?* will provide you with proper guidance and support.

As a parent, you can break the toxic patterns in this new generation of spenders and teach children what they really should know: how to exert control over their own lives. *Do I Look Like an ATM?* will help usher in a new culture in your family—a culture of abundance—and a healthy respect for money. Both are developed by becoming mindful of creating generational wealth.

Applying the information contained in *Do I Look Like an ATM?* is both a selfish and altruistic act on your part. By doing so, you will restore your own relationship with money through your children's relationship with money.

3

The ATM Generation

"If you must hold yourself up to your children as an object lesson, hold yourself up as a warning and not as an example." —GEORGE BERNARD SHAW

YOU MAY BE shocked to hear that it will cost $226,920 (not including college) for an average two-parent family to raise just one of its little darlings. According to the US Department of Agriculture, these costs are an increase of $60,000 from only a decade ago. And because you are making a sizable financial investment, teaching pumpkin how to be financially responsible is paramount in monitoring the costs of him living under your roof. After all, if your child didn't want everything he saw, perhaps your life would be less stressful, right?

My child just doesn't know just how good he has it.

You may be thinking, "If only my kids would stop acting as if money grew on trees and learn how to appreciate how hard I work to provide for them." Back in the olden days, you had to actually get up out of your lounge chair to change a television channel. When you were a child, you had three television stations and foil-covered rabbit ears to improve the reception. Now your child has a universal remote control designed to operate audio and video components and the home theater. Now your child has the audacity to not appreciate the monthly premium rates that you pay for access to three hundred television channels that no one ever watches.

When you were growing up, if you wanted surround sound, you and your buddies had to sit in the front row of the local Cineplex. There was no such thing as the Internet. And forget about e-mail and text messaging; you had to either wait for the mailman to arrive with an important letter or wait at home for a telephone call.

In the old days, you struggled to survive without caller ID. If your parents wanted to avoid a bill collector, they would make you lie: "My momma ain't home." Or your father would tell his friends to let the telephone ring three times, hang up, and then call back so he would know it was safe to pick up.

My child just doesn't know just how good he has it.

Well, who created your little cutie-pie? You did. Instead of making a blanket characterization of your child's money personality or focusing on the aspect that dismays you the most, let's dig deeper.

Nature and nurture are both powerful contributors to how a child interacts with money. For example, if a child is naturally frugal, his parents can teach him how to save money without being stingy or obsessive. Alternatively, if a child is overly generous to the point of giving away all of his money and toys to his classmates, parents can reinforce that spirit of giving, but also instruct him on how to be fair to himself. Parents can teach, no matter their child's personality, striking the right balance in his financial transactions while utilizing the principles of fair play.

First and foremost, parents should teach their children the value of money and how it will affect their present and their future. One easy way to do this is to play board games such as Monopoly and Acquire, which emphasize basic economics and stock market investments. Second, parents should consider giving allowances to their children, along with lessons on earning and managing their own bank accounts. Parents should allow their children to have part-time jobs or receive payment for certain household chores so they can develop and maintain a working and entrepreneurial spirit. Third, they should always have their children observe their online bank transactions and from time to time accompany them to the bank. While there, children should be shown how to make deposits and withdrawals, and the functions of bank employees should be explained in a way that they can understand. These hands-on field trips will get children invested in how money flows beyond their parents' wallets. This process will also familiarize children with finance and mathematics so that later in life numbers and computation do not intimidate them.

Parents also need to teach their children to become financially literate. They can do this by enrolling them in programs such as the Youth Investment Club, Camp Millionaire, the WorldofMoney.org Youth Financial Education Institute, or others across the United States. Among their peers, children can begin to learn about saving, investing, real estate, and the stock market.

Parents, acting as role models, need to show their children how they manage money in a positive way so that finances become part of the family culture and a natural and healthy part of children's psyches. Parents need to understand that, when it comes to money, success or failure is not defined by how much money one earns or how much one has lost. Success is one's ability to learn from mistakes, take strategic risks, and no matter what, continue to apply sound financial principles to one's daily life. Some days may bring feast, while others bring famine; some days may be a balance between the two extremes. The important point is that children must be socialized early on how to think and speak in wealthy terms. Young people will never learn the correct way to behave without being taught.

Take Robert Johnson, the founder of Black Entertainment Television, who sold his stake in the company for $3 billion. Later, after a 2002 divorce lowered his net worth, Johnson purchased an NBA franchise, the Charlotte Bobcats, and created the RLJ Companies, a collection of premier asset firms with substantial holdings in international real estate and entertainment.

Even after Johnson was not listed in *Forbes* in 2006, he continued to think and behave prosperously. He sought other investments and returned to the basics of earning, saving, and investing in growth-oriented investments and lucrative businesses. He has a wealth consciousness because of what he has learned about money and business.

On the other hand, according to the July 2011 issue of the *Review of Economics and Statistics,* the majority of million-dollar lottery winners lose or give away all of their prize money within five years because they were never taught how to manage money as children. This study further revealed that the majority of lottery winners did not use their awards to prevent bankruptcy, but instead only delayed the inevitable. Once parents understand this important point, they should feel less embarrassed about their own failings and more determined that their children will adopt a prosperous mindset.

What is the number-one emotional reason some black parents avoid engaging in a healthy way with the world of money? Parents report that, consciously and unconsciously, they are often surrounded by people, including family members, who encourage poor spending habits. In addition, parents have seen media images that portray black families as financially poor and struggling for survival resources. In fact, the media portrays the most successful black people as having merely achieved middle-class status, as if that is as far as African Americans can go financially.

Alternatively, the media often highlights blacks who squander millions. Therefore, parents often do not perceive money and wealth as being natural to their environments or even their families' futures. Some parents assume that financial stability will always be alien to them. Carla, mother of three, believes, "The black community is culturally mismatched with wealth because America's values are mismatched. Status in America is defined by money, and in other cultures, it is defined by values and your societal standing." Some African Americans value only what is highlighted in the media, and because they don't see enough affluent African Americans with real wealth, they are content being flashy and accumulating worthless trinkets.

With the exception of Oprah Winfrey and Robert Johnson, a number of self-made black billionaires remain out of the public eye but have been included over the years in *Forbes* magazine. In 2001 Johnson became the first African American billionaire, and the first black person, to be listed on any of *Forbes'* lists of the world's richest people. (Johnson's net worth is now valued at $500 million.) Parents can discuss with their children what strategies these men and women used to attain this financial success and how they can aspire to financial wealth.

The World's Black Billionaires (*Forbes*, 2011)

Name	Company	Net Worth (in billions)	Country of Residence
Aliko Dangote	Dangote Cement	$13.8	Nigeria
Mohammed Al-Amoudi	Midroc	$12.3	Saudi Arabia/ Ethiopia
Oprah Winfrey	Harpo	$2.8	United States
Mike Adenuga	Globacom	$2	Nigeria
Mo Ibrahim	Celtel	$1.8	United Kingdom

Contrary to popular belief, between 1983 and 2001, the number of black households with a net worth of $1 million or more increased 79 percent, from 61,000 households to 109,000. These black millionaires built their fortunes in large measure by owning their own businesses, such as real estate agencies, funeral homes, medical practices, construction companies, retail operations, and service sector businesses.

Parents admit that the subject of money is one of the most intimidating issues they will ever face. Most parents know their children should practice good spending habits. They are also aware that expert advice is available; but the thought of searching for outside resources can paralyze parents and prevent them from taking any action at all.

When did the ungrateful kid epidemic occur?

It seems like just yesterday you were carrying home the sweetest, most beautiful brown baby in the entire world. You dreamt of blissful moments, grade-school musicals, unconditional love, and heartfelt parental chats with your bundle of sunshine. You sang soulful lullabies while your perfect sugar lump tightly clutched your finger, gently cooing at the sound of your voice. You chuckled wistfully as lambkins grew enchanted by the clinking sound of your key ring. You envisioned your child's future milestones: high school prom, college graduation, and marriage.

All was well in the world. Your cutie-pie loved to hear the jingle of your pennies, nickels, dimes, and quarters. Overcome with curiosity, your dear toddler would insist on trying to eat your coins before you tossed them back into your wallet. "No, little bunny nose," you would warn protectively. "Those don't belong in your mouth." The Little People Christmas Train Set and the Giraffe Ring Stacker held temporary fascination, but nothing compared to the love your boo-boo felt for your money.

Your child also learned from observation that money could satisfy every desire. While you were wringing your hands trying to budget for next month's rent payment, your child bore witness as the adults in his world hovered over bills, played the Lotto, or complained about money issues. Your child may have heard you exclaim, "Do you think I'm made of money?" Or complain, "Lawd, this child wants me to buy everything she sees!" Or maybe you ordered, "Let me tell you something before we go into this store: I'm not buying you no more toys! So, don't ask! Do you hear me?"

Later, when it came time for Sweet Pea to board the school bus en route to her first day of kindergarten, you openly wept over the brawls you and your sweetie-pie had in aisle six of the local megastore, where not even former president Jimmy Carter could have brokered a peace deal. Explaining to your sweetie-pie that the Xbox GameFly was not coming home to compete with the untouched *That's So Raven* doll made you question your sanity.

The "I don't have any money!" lament was not effective because your child was with you when you paid for the rental furniture, and then your child pouted until his lips almost fell off because he felt that you deceived him. You explained, "I'm not wasting my money on no foolishness!" when you knew you were leasing a seventy-inch flat-screen television to watch your premium cable package. On the other hand, you might have purchased the Transformers Real Gear Robot to assuage your guilt, which rose out of your desire to provide your child with toys that you did not own growing up.

Any of these scenarios sound familiar?

Millions of parents like you are being hoodwinked every day and are drowning in fear and frustration. You may believe that your little angel lacks the capacity to learn the financial realities of the world. "Seems like everything I say goes in one ear and out of the other," many parents have mumbled. After all, you have the evidence to support your beliefs. You might join the parental chorus lamenting, "If I had a nickel for every time my child hollered, 'Gimme,' 'Can I have,' or 'I want,' I could be a retired tycoon on a Caribbean island."

To their peril, African American parents were never warned about the existence of an insidious set of genes in their precious babies—the dreaded Gimme Genome. Every day your teenager bombards you with endless requests for the latest gadget or CD or the current fashion styles, with their accompanying high price tags. "Can't he see how hard I work?" you think. "Does he think that money grows on trees? When will he ever learn to appreciate the roof over his head, the food he eats, and the clothes on his back? Will he ever be satisfied?"

The answer is *no*.

If you are like most parents, you are wondering what happened to your beloved darling of yesteryear. Don't worry—the hospital did not

Seven-year-old boy in the supermarket: "Mom, can I show you what I would want you to buy me if you were in a good mood?"

send the wrong baby home with you. Millions of black children like your own are coming of age in the exact same way.

Parents, you can give your child ultimate, empowering love by teaching them the tools to respect and manage money, the financial tools you were never given. Your support and direction lie within the pages of this book.

4

The Financial Bamboozle

"Too many people spend money they haven't earned, to buy things they don't want, to impress people they don't like." —Will Smith

REALITY CHECK: THIS is not torture. The following pages have not been created to squeeze enjoyment from your child's life. The information contained within is not designed to turn you or your child into a miser or a financial monk. However, these pages *will* tell the unvarnished truth. Here it is: you and your child are being tricked out of your money.

I hate to be the bearer of bad news, but your children are constantly being subliminally tricked out of understanding money. And depending on your child's money personality, he or she might be dragging you and your other family members along for the ride. You see, until this moment, you all had your heads in the sand and were willing participants on a reckless train ride toward bankruptcy and mounting debt. Until now, you and your children were having a party that would rival Brazil's annual Carnival.

Depending upon your family's financial culture, together you have been spending more than you earned, making 50 percent of your purchases on credit cards, saving little or no money, and living pay-check to paycheck. You are probably terrified about how you will sup-port yourself when you retire or if someone in the family suffers a medical emergency. Yet still, you and your family might be the first ones at Black Friday sales and have at least fifty brand-name products as well as clothes with the labels of enough fashion designers to con-vene a Madison Avenue convention in their honor.

If you totaled the costs of all of your excess expenditures from the last two years, the amount would dwarf what is in your savings account—that is, if you have a savings account. But I will address this idea in chapter 9. For now, allow me to tap you on your shoulder and make an announcement: your children have been socialized to make *other* people wealthy. Please pardon my harshness, but that is as real as it gets. They have been socialized to not only make other people wealthy, but to make those people's children and their children's chil-dren wealthy as well.

How does that feel? Not so good, I trust.

Since we are keeping it real, allow me to continue. Many of your child's favorite celebrities, who have mishandled their finances because they were never taught otherwise, are leading the way off the financial cliff. Rap artists and celebrities are paid vast amounts to tout brands, under a hypnotic beat, convincing their audiences that they are the scum of the earth unless they are wearing the same jackets and sneak-ers or using the same phones, which, incidentally, were produced by children like yours, for pennies, on the other side of the world.

You've all been hoodwinked.

You might be protesting right now, thinking that clearly I am misin-formed. Your kids might be listening to Wu-Tang Clan's "C.R.E.A.M.," in which the chorus says, "Cash rules everything around me / C.R.E.A.M. / Get the money / Dolla dolla bill y'all." And you know what? Wu-Tang is correct. But once they "get the money," do any of these musical art-ists know how to keep and grow that money so that their children and their children's children are financially prosperous?

Should their financial educations begin and end with a musical track? Should your pursuit of money resemble a cocker spaniel gulping water from his bowl?

■ Make It Rain

Fat Joe's "Make It Rain" is the anthem of decadent disrespect for and display of money. The scenario from the 2006 song plays out with African American males in nightclubs throwing bills at half-naked strippers or out into screaming audiences.

At rapper Rick Ross's birthday party one year, $1 million was thrown on the floor. After the million dollars was thrown down, a Brink's armored truck rolled in with even more money. Lance Williams, PhD, associate professor and assistant director of the Jacob H. Carruthers Center for Inner City Studies at Northeastern Illinois University, reports, "This depiction of making it rain [shows] black youth, even if they have money, with a sophistication so low that they are willing to flagrantly throw it away, believing that money is nothing." Dr. Williams argues that black youth culture is being exploited and commoditized by entertainment corporations for their own benefit.

Williams continues, "For the corporations, their influence over black youth is not limited to extracting over $500 million out of the black community each year. There has been an erosion of the values of the resources that go along with the expression in the rap music industry, which is an emphasis on owning material things, a stark difference from the early days of hip-hop, where the emphasis was on conveying a positive message and having fun. Now it is about flaunting lots of jewelry and people and artists bragging about the latest clothes. It makes sense that this is happening because the corporations that are promoting these products are the same ones who control the music industry."

The rap music industry is itself a product of the music industry, which is a part of general mass media; and in particular, the problem comes with the corporatization of music. I agree with critics who see media outlets and corporations not just as moneymaking companies but as key participants in the industry of cultural production. The commoditization of hip-hop and rap music has arisen because of a larger effort by corporations to produce or reproduce culture, especially black youth culture.

Black youth have a purchasing power of $500 million per year, so if corporations can create a culture of consumerism among black youth, these companies then have access to a large amount of money. Marketing companies recognize that if they can get black youth in the United States to endorse particular products, then other youth in America and around the world will follow their lead and purchase these products, too. If black youth decide that a product is hot, then white youth, who have even greater purchasing power, will see it as cool because they see black youth as a model of what is cool, hot, popular, and worthy of emulation.

One could argue that the genius of young people is always commercialized. However, black youth are the only demographic, on such a global scale, whose creativity and behaviors are co-opted, mass-produced, and then sold back to them at inflated rates.

Collectively, black youth leave $500 million in other people's pockets over the course of each year of consumption. Now compare that with what is in your savings account and your investment portfolio. And black youth don't even recognize their own purchasing power; they simply become walking billboards for products that make money for other people. Merely looking financially successful reigns supreme over creating a strategic plan for achieving financial success.

Still not convinced? Dr. Williams explains it this way:

> Youth are intoxicated by the amount of money that they think many of these artists make. The following chart shows how much the majority of rap artists earn from each CD.

Average CD cost	$15.95
Record company	$4.46
Retailer	$3.00
Distributor	$3.50
Songwriter	$1.00
Producer	$1.00
Manufacturer	$1.00
Artist	**$1.43**

Being a music artist is cool, but if you are making $1.43 [from] each CD, you ain't no pimp, dude. You are not a hustler; you are getting played in that relationship. Rap artists proclaim that they are a pimp, but they are not getting the largest percent. So if Jay-Z makes $30 million, that sounds like a lot of money, but the rest of his pie is eaten up by old white men who are making $300 million. So, why are we so happy that Jay-Z made $30 million? Black youth need to want to be the owner of the record label and own the song publishing rights to their songs. You want to be the distributor, not just the artist.

Many companies use black rappers and black youth in general to give the impression that the rappers are actually in control when actually, as Dr. Williams explains, "they are a pass through, and they are a face of the company. Unfortunately, black youth are exploited for their creativity and their images, while others reap mind-numbing profits. Because black youth are seen as the poster representatives for these record companies, they rarely receive sustained community pressure. Those who are ignorant of how this financial system works will become a victim of it."

Questlove, a member of hip-hop group the Roots, stated in an interview, "Hip-hop is full of tall tales. Eighty percent of those people we thought were living the life were not. And that is real. I didn't know that Bentley was leased, that house was rented. Watch *MTV Cribs* and the truth starts to reveal itself. I know a very high-profile person in the hip-hop nation that only has $1,000 to their name."

So, what does this discussion of the materialism in rap music have to do with you and your family? As a parent you need to understand that international music corporations recognize how influential these messages are in your child's consciousness. The marketing of hundreds of products by their idols has your children craving sneakers, cell phones, and clothes, and is making them feel that they are worthless unless those products are hanging from their bodies or in their closets.

■ True Power Comes from Within

If it could be said that any one recording artist created the blueprint for building wealth, one would need to look no further than Percy Miller, formerly known as Master P. "I have not programmed my son Romeo to be a financial thug," he explained. "I programmed him for generational wealth."

Reared in the worst housing project in New Orleans, Miller used his street savvy and recognized that any relationship a person enters into regarding money is one of dominance and exploitation. In his 2007 book *Guaranteed Success: When You Never Give Up*, Miller writes, "If you don't know what you are worth, then you don't know what you are truly capable of accomplishing. It's impossible to tap into your ultimate potential when you place a low value on your self-worth."

As an example, he talked about pursuing his career in the record business. At one point, he was down to his last $500; and the rent, the car note, his kids' tuition, and every other bill were due. Along came an offer to buy the rights to his name and his record label, No Limit Records. The label had that name because Miller's grandfather had once told him, "There is no limit to your self-worth. Your self-worth is priceless."

So when Interscope Records offered him $1 million to sign a contract, Miller's first thought was that the offer meant he was worth ten to twenty times more. Far too many artists, finding themselves down to their last handful of cash, would have taken anything in order to get a deal. But Miller turned down the offer, and within a couple of years he was earning over $2 million selling his own CDs from the trunk of his car. Furthermore, Interscope cut Miller a new deal that gave him a larger percentage share than any other artist.

Miller later blew millions of dollars coping with tax problems and on monetary gifts, but because he possesses a prosperous mindset, he recouped his financial losses by creating other companies. Now he spreads his message of building wealth and financial literacy through a nationwide speaking tour and credits his mindset shift to the writings of Robert Kiyosaki, of *Rich Dad, Poor Dad* fame, and Donald Trump.

■ The Cost of Looking Good

If your child is like most black teens, he or she spends 6 percent more per month than the average American young person, averaging about $428 monthly.[1] Yearly, black teens spend more on items such as clothing, jewelry, computer software, and athletic footwear than other US teens. Even if your kid is more frugal than most, Madison Avenue advertisers still bank on the fact that black youth are a powerful force in the US market. Twelve- to seventeen-year-olds spent $112.5 billion in 2003 alone. Apparently youth from so-called low-income households spent more than other young people.

One more point you need to examine: according to a 2007 US Census Bureau report, the median household income for black families is $33,916, while that of whites is $54,920. For Asians the figure is $66,103, and for Hispanics, $38,679.

---

1. Pepper Miller and Herb Kemp, *What's Black About It? Insights to Increase Your Share of a Changing African-American Market* (Ithaca, NY: Paramount Market Publishing, 2005).

What does this mean? Black people are earning the least but spending the most.

Other than magic, how does that make sense? Black people—and black youth in particular—are more than willing to go into debt with credit card companies and with personal loans in order to consume products and apparel that they think make them look affluent. Mind you, I said, "make them look affluent," not "actually make them affluent." This trend did not just begin with your children. The willingness to pay any cost to look good began with your parents and their parents. Yes, this has been going on for generations.

Today, your children are mirroring the spending habits of the adults in their lives and abiding by media dictates about how they should look and how they should spend your money. Without strategizing about how to effectively use money as a family, you perpetuate black stereotypes and willingly forfeit the opportunity to save for your kids' college educations or to purchase real estate.

Have you taken a vow of poverty? Are you determined to make other people rich? Are you determined to never have money to weather life's financial storms? If so, you are not modeling the behaviors of the rich and financially responsible; instead you are mirroring the behaviors of those with a poverty mindset.

It's your choice. Will you lead your family toward poverty or begin building a sound financial foundation?

5

The Problem with the Joneses

Teresa's Story

Teresa is a divorced fifty-two-year-old high school teacher living with her four children in Jamaica, Queens.

"My children did the happy dance when I opened the door to our new $1.5 million brownstone in Bed-Stuy, Brooklyn. Everyone in my circle of friends was jumping on the bandwagon. Every day, someone I knew was buying a home and often was rewarded with something extra, like a new dining room set. I saw leaders from our community urging everyone to seize this opportunity. Tears came to my eyes when they talked about how our children would benefit, just like rich families, in buying a house now. One community leader in particular had lobbied the banks so they could create mortgages that were accessible to families such as mine.

"Despite my bad credit, I was able to secure [a] no-money-down mortgage. And we also received 100 percent financing. In fact, most of us were in the same condition. But we were told that 2002 was the time to buy our own home. Buying my own home—unlike everyone else in my family, I had achieved the American dream. There was a buying frenzy. There were home-buying conventions all over the city. So, like everyone else, I jumped at the opportunity, and so did many other people that I know.

"I was so happy before everything started to change. But, like my friends and neighbors, I wanted to own my own business. They were withdrawing equity out of their homes and opening their own businesses. Like them, I always dreamed of owning my own café, specializing in breakfast and brunch. I believed that I needed to prepare for the next chapter of my life, after retiring from the Board of Education.

"My then-husband joined with our neighbors in a real estate business, buying and flipping houses. Everything was going OK for a while, but it seemed the more I invested in the renovations for the cafe, the more money I needed to spend. But then, when all of our neighbors started buying boats, minivans, vacation homes, cars for their children's high school graduations, new wardrobes, and taking annual dream trips around the world, there was nothing to worry about because, as we were told, the value of our homes was going up, up, up! And the value did! If we needed more money, all we had to do was refinance. And we did—twice.

"And everything went well for a while. I doted on my children. Whatever their friends bought or wanted to buy, my children owned the same item or had the same experience soon thereafter. It came to a point where I stopped asking how everyone else was able to spend so much. I wanted me and my children to be just like everyone else. Everything seemed in order. We were not thieves in the night stealing mortgages, giving our children everything they wanted. The nationally regarded bank was more than happy to grant us extended lines of credit so that we could purchase whatever we wanted or charged on our credit card.

"From my husband's income and new promotion as a technical supervisor with the telephone company and my income teaching and tutoring on the weekend, we knew that we could afford our adjustable mortgage and our growing expenses. It took the city marshal sneaking, in the dead of night, to repossess my Land Rover and my children watching me disguise my voice when the credit card [company] phoned demanding payment for me to accept that over all of these years, I had been trying to keep up with the Joneses. In my case, whenever I saw my neighbor make a large purchase, I would feel compelled to do the same. In spite of the fact that my financial life was a train wreck, I would find some way to make sure that my family was perceived as having achieved a high standard of living. Then I would have the audacity to chastise my children by telling them that they needed to stop behaving as though money grew on trees. What a hypocrite I have become!

"While I was encouraging them, through my actions, to pick from the money tree, my elderly father shook his head in disgust. He never understood having a million dollars in debt, when we did not have a million dollars to pay it back. My father never understood that my husband and I lived without a budget. He never heard of the words 'adjustable rates,' 'sub-prime,' 'flipping,' and 'APR.' I had, but I ignored how their meaning would apply to my life and everyone I knew.

"Of course, I ignored my father's voice of reason. This was a new day, and everyone was doing this, so it must be OK. And I would be damned if my children went without. My children were enrolled in the best private schools and met the best people.

"Then, as quickly as our house of cards was created, it fell. First, my husband was laid off from his job. He felt that his real estate business would perform well. It did not. Each evening, my friends would phone with similar stories of layoffs or firings or that their companies went bankrupt. I heard stories of friends having to withdraw their children from private schools.

"Soon the dreaded word 'foreclosure' crept into our conversations. Though it was happening to everyone, in my mind I could not believe that Lady Luck would affect my family in the same way. But it did.

"My children do not understand what is real. They are bitter that I had to enroll them in a public school, away from their well-to-do friends, in a new school district. They hated that we had to sell their cars, our boat, and [short-sell] the house.

"We are now renting a two-bedroom apartment, and the credit card companies must phone at least four times a day. The hardest part about this situation is that my marriage crumbled. My husband disappeared, as he could not accept that he was unable to provide for his family financially. When I explained that millions of Americans were in the exact same situation, he could not hear me and just moved in with his sister."

THE TIME HAS come to identify those shadowy financial influences in our lives: let's call them the Joneses. Many of them drive around in giant SUVs, dangling keys to other vehicles that they have not quite paid for, loaded up with material goods for which they are paying exorbitant interest rates to their credit card companies, all the while talking or texting on the latest cell phones. You might not be able to tell by looking at them, but the Joneses are deeply in debt. If you stop to ask them how they are doing financially, if they are truly honest, they will tell you that they are just barely getting by. The Joneses might also tell you that their debt exceeds anything their own parents could ever have imagined.

You and your children may have been given the tools to flaunt money as symbols of a wealthy lifestyle rather than being educated for wealth accumulation. The days when our parents saved and then paid cash for big- and small-ticket items are long gone. Adults now teach our children that they are entitled to have expensive trinkets that in the past were for the exclusive use of the rich and famous. Our children live on a new frontier of consumerism. Conspicuous consumption has brought the lifestyles of the rich and famous to our children's consciousness and is often sanctioned by parental behavior.

The Joneses are a fairly cordial family, but their negative influence may put you on the fast track to bankruptcy court. On the outside, the Joneses are the average African American family, perhaps with 2.5 children, and married or never married or recently divorced. Statistically, at least two adults per household are employed. In the black community, as well as in towns and cities throughout America, neighbors participate in the age-old jockeying for position that plays out in the accumulation of material goods and in comparing themselves to their neighbors, people that they might not even know. People on the Joneses' treadmill perceive those who fail to participate in this mindless consumerism to be culturally and economically inferior. Parents often use the Joneses as the barometer for their own self-esteem, an assessment of them as parents, and a way to show the world that their family is financially prospering, even when they are not.

Our children are being socialized into believing that greed is good and that mindless spending is as necessary as oxygen. Our children have rarely heard the word "frugal" or would consider being so corny, boring, and nerdy. Just witness the facial expression of the average child when her parents tell her that they cannot purchase another toy. It's almost like they're having an asthma attack!

The Joneses, who, let's remember, are broke, have on average four credit cards (with huge balances), wear famous designers and twenty pounds of jewelry at once, and lease a new automobile every year. The Joneses invest more in their hairstyles and their apparel than in their children's education, and they believe that homeownership—without so much as a down payment—is a constitutional right. The Joneses are the Pied Pipers of Excess and are leading you into a financial purgatory, while our children are witnesses and future participants. Many of our children believe the Joneses are to be idolized; for them, just wearing expensive jewelry means they have ascended into the world of wealth.

A careful review of the chart on the next page shows that the Joneses in the African American community are putting $1.1 trillion a year into laying a financial foundation of depreciation, purchasing items with zero appreciative value. According to Target Market News, with the exception of home expenditures, the top ten expenditures in African American

> "The thing that impresses me most about America is the way parents obey their children."
>
> —EDWARD VIII,
> DUKE OF WINDSOR

households are items that have no resale value. The Joneses have wooed your children's consciousness into financial quicksand. Now it is up to parents to seize the wheel and chart a new course.

The Top Ten Expenditures in Black Households, 2009

Housing and Related Charges	$166.3 billion
Education	$71 billion
Food	$65.3 billion
Cars and Trucks: New and Used	$31.5 billion
Apparel Products and Services	$26.9 billion
Health Care	$23.9 billion
Telephone Services	$17.2 billion
Households Furnishings and Equipment	$12.9 billion
Travel, Transportation, and Lodging	$6.4 billion
Consumer Electronics	$4.5 billion
Computers	$3.5 billion
Tobacco Products and Smoking Supplies	$3.1 billion
Toys, Games, and Pets	$2.4 billion

According to Target Market News, black families respond to their economic plight with expenditures on products and services that improve their homes and lifestyles instead of their investment and retirement portfolios. Black families used limited incomes to make their homes more comfortable. In 2009, appliance expenditures grew 27 percent to $2.2 billion, while consumer electronics purchases increased by 32 percent to $4.5 million. Despite economic trends, black families rank seventeenth among world economies in comparable gross national income. They represent a powerful economic block but have yet to wield this power for the benefit of their own families.

■ All That Glitters Isn't Gold

In the African American community, the influence of the Joneses is perpetuated by the images of reality television stars, athletes, and musicians that fill your child's daily entertainment quota. They also serve to fill an emotional emptiness, a need to feel valued. And many parents are right there next to their children, waiting in line to get the latest gadget, sign up for access to the highest-speed Internet service, buy the newest television with the largest screen, and purchase the most coveted brands of jewelry. Nancy, age forty-one, confides, "Giving money and things to my children gives me joy, and when I can't, I feel upset, like I am letting them down." Like many parents, Nancy believes that her inability to meet the desires of her children reflects on her ability to parent. Yet her style of parenting blurs for children the stark distinction between needs and wants, between necessities and luxuries. Nancy also makes endless, unwise expenditures to nourish her own emotional insecurities rather than making ones that will benefit her children.

Modern-day parents regard certain items that would have been considered luxuries by our parents as absolute necessities. Even purchasing luxury sport-utility vehicles is justified as a necessity under the guise of safety. There are now so many of these behemoths on the highway that it appears as though the only way to be secure during a financial crash is to make sure you and your children are driving one, too.

This reality is borne out by the Pew Research Center, which reports that 84 percent of African Americans are not saving enough money for an emergency or for their retirement, as compared with whites (74 percent) or Hispanics (78 percent). This relationship persists even after differences in income are taken into account. At the same time, the expenditures of nearly nine in ten African Americans (87 percent) earning $50,000 or more continue to increase, even as they admit they are not saving enough.

Weekly manicures and pedicure services, hair weaves, monthly spa facials, unused gym memberships, expensive fashion and accessories, private contractors, and landscapers are clearly not necessities, yet they top the acquisition lists of some parents. A rational assessment

Why We Do It

A variety of factors drive consumption:

- The desire to show off our acquisitions
- Craving what other people have
- Prolific advertising and product placement
- A society that favors instant gratification over sustained hard work
- Access to easy, often high-interest, credit

by parents to determine if these items are necessities or luxuries can lead to tremendous savings and teach children to make the same judgments.

Many items that were seen as fads or that did not exist in the 1990s have recently catapulted onto the necessity list, a shift that stems from a feeling of entitlement. According to a 2006 survey entitled "Necessity or Luxury" by the Pew Research Center, 33 percent of Americans now view cable or satellite TV as a necessity. In 1996, that number was 17 percent. Also, 51 percent now cannot live without a home computer, up from 26 percent in 1996.

The following items are considered necessities for each specified percentage of Americans:

- Cell phone: 49 percent
- High-speed Internet: 29 percent
- Designer apparel: 15 percent
- Luxury automobile: 10 percent
- Flat-screen TV: 5 percent
- iPod or tablet computer: 3 percent

Influenced by the Joneses, financially fragile parents are eating at the trough of gluttonous consumerism and have completely flipped priorities and values. Thus it does not require a great leap of logic to surmise that our children are simply mirroring the same behavior. It is difficult to resist the seductive images propagated by the media, which repeatedly tell you that your family must have more than you can actually pay for—and that you must instantly have whatever you desire. You are entitled, society tells you.

▪ Celebrity Joneses

When the threat of a National Football League lockout loomed in 2011, many professional players living luxury lifestyles experienced financial fumbles. A multimillionaire NBA player (who apparently managed his finances more prudently) promised to help his cash-strapped NFL counterparts out of their financial problems during the lockout. Stories like these remind us that not only are the Joneses broke or temporarily without funds, their celebrity counterparts are, too. Evolving out of the 1980s television program *Lifestyles of the Rich and Famous*, newer so-called reality television offers a similar slant. In 2000, MTV debuted a television series called *MTV Cribs* that toured the homes of famous celebrities. In 2004, however, it was reported that some of the rappers appearing on the television program were not in fact the true owners of the homes on display. This revelation did not put brakes on the trend, though, and in 2009, *Teen Cribs* aired, featuring the homes of regular teenagers, without the celebrity element. This was followed by *My Super Sweet 16*, which featured the opulent parties provided by parents for their spoiled children. These shows taught young people that fame and consumerism reign supreme. Similarly, the highly rated *Real Housewives*, *Basketball Wives*, and *Love and Hip Hop* franchises dominate cable programming, supposedly to provide insight into the perfect lives of rich women. These financially lucrative franchises flaunt materialistic, ill-tempered, tantrum-throwing women and their children, who have no clear sources of income but live in gated communities, drive luxury cars, and wear designer clothes.

Each week, the casts of these shows and others like them offer profound lessons on how to devalue money. The true reality is that if parents are determined to keep up with the Joneses, the Kardashians, or the Housewives, their children will model the same financial misbehavior. Many adult viewers compare themselves to these people and set their own bar of success accordingly. But many of the cast members are struggling financially, getting divorced, missing out on healthy relationships with their children, and facing foreclosure or bankruptcy. The Internal Revenue Service and collection agencies became regular parts of their lives as they and their children drowned in extravagance. While attempting to bolster their self-esteem and outrun the Joneses, cast members also faced civil lawsuits and had to eventually admit they did not own the homes and automobiles shown on their shows. Still, they seemed content to continue to teach their children, through their own actions, how to squander their earnings.

■ Your Child Wants You, Not Things

"Children will not remember you for the material things you provided but for the feeling that you cherished them." —ROBERT EVANS

Drowning your child in material goods will never reduce any feelings of vulnerability you may experience as a parent. Ignoring your child's financial education will not teach her how to save and delay gratification. When children are taught the true value of items such as the ones on the Target Market News expenditures list, many are no longer interested in the products. For example, when children learn that there is a high markup between the actual cost of producing a sneaker and the retail price, and when they hear about how shareholders of sneaker companies receive dividends from the profits of these companies, many lose interest in possessing these trendy items. One year, during the Youth Financial Education Institute, when teenagers were asked to name the brands that their friends would flaunt during the impending school year, they enthusiastically shouted out twelve well-known brands. The room grew silent, however, when they were taught that powerful, influential advertising campaigns were the reason they knew these brands and when they learned that they were being socially engineered into remaining loyal consumers instead of savers, entrepreneurs, producers, and investors.

When children are taught that they must use their allowance for what they want instead of using their parents' credit card to foot the bill, many of them quickly lose interest in purchasing those items. Giving to our children what we believe our parents should have provided for us is not the path toward raising financially responsible young people. Our children should be taught how to earn their money and delay gratification by saving over the long term to make purchases. Will your little darling accept the $50,000 BMW for his high school graduation present? Absolutely! But when we chronicle our lives and the time spent with our own parents, we recognize that the treasured moments came not through gifts we can no longer remember but from the time and empathy our parents gave us. Keeping up with the Joneses to assuage our emotional needs will not groom an empowered child. Instead of things, children want their parents—even if they seem totally annoyed by the idea. Children want to be valued for their individual talents and goals and have their parents there in the role of supportive cheerleaders.

Are parents to become misers and never allow their children the pleasure of spending on a desired item? Absolutely not. However, a balance must be sought so that a child recognizes that nothing in your relationship is more important than your mutual love, guidance, and protection. Many mothers and fathers today believe that they are not good enough parents unless they are coddling their children and shielding them from so-called adult responsibilities. Of course, parents want to give their children all the pleasures and opportunities that they did not have. They want to shield their children from life's very real worries and stresses. But in doing so, they inadvertently also deny them the chance to learn the skills that will enable them to become self-reliant.

Young people report, however, that while they temporarily delight in gifts, they most long for emotional bonding with their parents.

Emotional bonding supersedes consumerism, and accordingly, children should not be allowed to have everything that they say they want the instant they want it. What children report they want on a deeper level are the quiet moments during which their parents are compassionate and affectionate and the opportunity to spend quality time alone with them. Through these interactions, parents can get to know their children's financial personalities and strengthen their emotional relationships at the same time.

Parents need to raise children who are comfortable in their own skins and who could care less what the Jones children are doing or wearing. Instead, parents can teach their children about financially successful Americans such as Madam C. J. Walker, Steve Jobs, and Oseola McCarty. Never heard of Ms. McCarty? Born in 1908, Oseola McCarty was employed as a laundry woman for the majority of her life. Though she never became a millionaire, by the time of her death, she had amassed and donated $150,000 to the University of Southern Mississippi to provide financial assistance to students in need. Though she dropped out of school in the sixth grade, Oseola McCarty was taught to save money by her mother. She did not understand the purpose of being extravagant. She never owned an automobile, and she walked everywhere she went. She did not subscribe to a newspaper or magazine and owned a black-and-white television. When her mother and aunt died, Ms. McCarty deposited what they had left for her in a savings account. It was late in her life when friends convinced her to purchase two small window air conditioners for her house. Her will provided 10 percent of her estate to her church and 30 percent to three of her relatives; 60 percent of her monies went to the University of Southern Mississippi. "I just want the scholarship to go to some child who needs it, to whoever is not able to help their children," Ms. McCarty is quoted as saying. "I'm too old to get an education, but they can."

Ms. McCarty told Frank McKenzie, a local attorney for whom she had done laundry, that she did not want anyone to try to convince her to change how she had decided to distribute her sizable savings. Thus

---

Why Parents Do It

- Parents keep up with the Joneses because they have not learned how to challenge the materialist culture around them. Face it—parents were once children too, and they may or may not have overcome their own challenges in facing peer pressure in adulthood.

- Financially fragile parents feel that they must compensate to provide material goods for their children so that they both feel as though they are measuring up to the Joneses. And the less time parents spend with their children, the more they tend to indulge them financially.

- Consumerism and a lack of family time are deeply embedded in the cultures of many so-called rich countries.

McKenzie created an irrevocable trust, which prevents a grantor from changing one's beneficiaries after the document is notarized. She also gave the bank responsibility for managing her funds.

In 1998, Ms. McCarty was awarded an honorary degree from the University of Southern Mississippi, the first of its kind given to an African American. Harvard University bestowed an honorary doctorate, and Bill Clinton honored her with a Presidential Citizens Medal, the nation's highest civilian award. In a letter to Ms. McCarty, the president wrote, "Hillary and I were moved by your gift to the University of Southern Mississippi. Your unselfish deed is a remarkable example of the spirit and ingenuity that made America great."

Together with your child, examine your current needs and wants—and most of all, your values. Disregard societal values that focus on materialism. Consider these suggestions:

- ❯ Discuss the finances of various celebrities. Explain or research how various celebrities' businesses operate (including the role of employees).

❯ Discuss with your child any possible peer pressure she may experience to wear or own trendy items.

❯ Review Christmas and birthday traditions. Discuss the reason behind the seasons. If necessary, consider adjusting the family's desire to overspend during chaotic holidays.

From a practical perspective, spending money on products with depreciating values may gladden your child's heart temporarily, but in reality, doing so is unnecessary for your child's well-being and your family's financial stability. Children have an insatiable desire to possess whatever advertising campaigns promote. Know that your child will survive without these things and will learn how to become prosperous as they lose their tendency to crave everything that they see.

■ Assignments

❯ Honestly document occurrences when you purchased an item shortly after you were aware that someone else had made the same purchase.

❯ Write down why you made each purchase.

❯ What celebrity or designer do you model your purchases after? Which designer or retailer do you value over the others?

❯ Document the details of each of these purchases. What was the original purchase price? What is the current resale value? How has that purchase positively or negatively affected your life?

❯ Most people do not use all of the features on their smartphones. Does your family really need all of the television channels that you pay for? Is there a less costly package available? Do you really need to lease your automobile? Can your monthly car payment be reduced so that the savings can be contributed toward your retirement?

Parents should not worry about what other people have. Your money is your money. Show your children what you value by using your money wisely.

■ The Gray Areas

In developing financially responsible children, parents need to begin by discussing the definitions of and distinction between needs and wants. Avoiding this task will foster family discord that stems from children's constant purchase requests.

- ❥ Need: Something one requires to survive, such as food, shelter, water, or clothing.
- ❥ Want: Something one desires but does not need to survive—for example, an Apple MacBook Pro laptop or thirty different pairs of sneakers.
- ❥ Priority: Something that takes precedent over other things.

In a world where many adults demand instant gratification, it is no wonder that our children focus on satisfying their wants and lack appreciation when their needs are provided for by their parents. One would think that adults and society in general would have a better handle on this issue. Intellectually, parents faced with mounting household expenses understand the difference. Whether you are grocery shopping or packing for a trip, the difference between needs and wants is fairly apparent. However, sometimes parents may blur the line between needs and wants, leaving their children to follow their unintentional example. Children are often very clear about what they want. However, the emotion-backed urgency with which children beg parents for a variety of fleeting desires often blurs the stark distinction between needs and wants. Many parents are pressured by their children's unrelenting nagging, and because they love them, they falter, resulting in closets and lives that are filled with more wants than needs.

■ The Whining Factor

According to the August 2011 issue of the *Journal of Children and Media*, researchers from the Johns Hopkins Bloomberg School of Public

Health found that children's manipulative whining could cause their parents to make ill-informed purchases and serve high-sugar, low-nutrition foods. Furthermore, in 1998 Western International Media reported that 40 percent of parent purchases of entertainment and fast food and 30 percent of home video purchases were the result of giving in to their children's whining. Spurred on by advertising campaigns, children have learned not to take no for an answer. The Center for a New American Dream says that, "on average, young people aged 12–17 report asking nine times for products they've seen advertised before their parents give in and let them have what they want. More than 10% admitted to asking their parents more than fifty times."

Clearly, parents want to make their children happy; they may even believe that feeding into their materialism may achieve that goal. However, according to the 2005 book *What Do Children Need to Flourish? Conceptualizing and Measuring Indicators of Positive Development*, materialistic children do not flourish. Instead, they were found to have lower self-esteem, be less happy, and express anxiety. These children also showed less generosity and resisted contributing to charitable organizations.

However, you can take action against their materialism. Assign to your child the task of reviewing monthly household bills. Have your child calculate the total amount due for household expenses. Ask her for ideas about ways that your family can save more money. In a calm tone, discuss how you plan to allocate your income to pay household expenses. Further, explain that proper money management does not come from ignoring one's finances.

While grocery shopping, discuss what distinguishes a *need* from a *want* and what a *priority* is. Talk with your child about setting a long-term savings goal for your family as a whole and for each family member. Periodically require your child to earn the money needed to pay for a somewhat expensive item he wants. Show your child examples of teen millionaire entrepreneurs and philanthropists. Encourage her to adopt their mindsets and behaviors.

REMEMBER WHEN YOU were little and you were entirely too concerned with what your friend had or what your sibling was doing? Your mom told you, "Don't worry about others. Mind your own business and worry about yourself." That's a lesson we all seem to forget as we get older. We unintentionally teach our children that if you have a nest egg stashed away or a seemingly endless supply of cash, you should by all means spend away. But in truth, if you're concerned about the future, you need to curb your spending today.

Take a page from low-income America and limit your assumed "needs." The same survey that found 3 percent of adults considered iPods a necessity also discovered that the less a person earned, the fewer items he or she listed as actual necessities—items that no one could live without.

■ Perspective Exercises

Needs and Wants Household Inventory Chart

Family members should conduct a "needs and wants" inventory of household possessions and then share and discuss the results.

Needs and Wants Household Inventory Chart

Needs	Wants

Global Needs and Wants

Children should research a locale and then discuss what the needs and wants could be for the families who reside there.

Global Harvest Chart

Country	Occupation	Family Needs	Family Wants
Barbados	Cruise Director		
Brazil	Fisherman		
Canada	Educator		
China	Factory Worker		
Ethiopia	Prime Minister		
France	Café Owner		
India	Unemployed		
Jamaica	Potterymaker		
Sudan	Herder		
United States	Attorney		
United States	Farmer		

■ Delayed Gratification Strategy

Because our society promotes instant gratification, many parents may have to reflect upon their own habits of satisfying their desires. This attitude could appear in parents in a number of ways. Ask yourself:

- ❯ Do you feel you must possess the latest, fastest gadgets?
- ❯ Are you always seeking the next new product?
- ❯ Have you ever felt impatient when receiving an e-mail took five seconds longer than usual?
- ❯ Do you feel you must purchase the latest-model automobile every year?
- ❯ Do you find it abhorrent to wear so-called out-of-style clothes?

- Do you feel competitive with other parents in your neighborhood? Do you feel that your family must match purchases made by other parents?

The Stanford marshmallow experiment was made famous in 1972 by professor Walter Mischel. The experimenter would leave a young child alone in a room with one marshmallow after promising him that if he waited fifteen minutes and did not eat the marshmallow, he would be rewarded with a second marshmallow. Children who delayed gratification by waiting fifteen minutes for a two-marshmallow payoff were found during a follow-up experiment fourteen years later to have higher grades and better SAT test scores. These young people also exhibited more assertiveness, self-reliance, dependability, trustworthiness, and academic competence, as well as greater abilities to cope with frustration and refrain from using alcohol and drugs.

On the other hand, the children who opted for instant gratification and ate the single marshmallow before the fifteen minutes had expired were found to be indecisive, stubborn, and impulsive. They also tended to be more envious of others, were poorer students, possessed lower self-image, were easily frustrated, and had more experience with drugs and alcohol.

■ Assignments

Parents can instill in their children the ability to delay gratification through the following actions:

- Require that your child focus on community service, instead of fulfilling her self-esteem through materialism.
- Knowing that $150 billion is spent annually on powerful advertising, parents should reduce their children's television viewing time.
- Purchase a translucent piggy bank so that your child can see his savings accumulate.

❍ Share with your child real-life examples of things that take a long period to achieve—for example, a tree growing and producing fruit, making bread from scratch, training for a marathon, or sailing around the world.

❍ Keep in mind that the word "no" will not devastate your child. The more your little darling is prepared at home for being denied her requests, the far better she will be prepared for the real world.

❍ Teach your child how to wait for something that he desires. Set a time for treats, gifts, and other rewards so that your child does not become conditioned to believe that the world is obligated to bestow rewards at his whim.

❍ When your child announces that he really wants something, you should respond by asking, "If you borrow the money from me, how soon can I expect to be paid back, with interest?" Often children will decide that owning something loses its luster when they either have to spend their own money on it or return the payment to their parent.

❍ Ask your child to arrange her favorite possessions in her room. Then ask her how much money was spent on each item. Have your child total the amounts. Then say, "Was it worth it? Would you prefer to have the possessions or the money?"

Delayed gratification helps shape children into patient adults who are able to make long-term financial decisions. It helps teach them the difference between a need and a want.

Nurturing a child's understanding of the difference between needs and wants will also help them to embrace their "good life" as opposed to their "goods life." As children witness their parents prioritizing their expenditures, they will adopt the lessons they are being taught.

6

The Road to Travel

"Ye shall know the truth, and the truth shall make you free." —John 8:32

BEFORE LEAVING THE house, you gaze into a mirror to make sure that you are presentable. You make sure that your clothes are clean, your shoes are shined, your hair is neat, and your teeth are brushed. You invest considerable time and effort to make sure that you are dressed to impress. You want the world to see you as a successful person. And that's good—to a point.

How much time do you invest in dressing your financial picture? Making sure your retirement account is neat? Double-checking that your six-month emergency account is shined? Instead of reading department store advertisements, have you researched Bankrate.com to identify the highest available compound interest rate in your city? Have you dusted off your legal papers to make sure your estate documents are in order?

A little scary, isn't it? And very personal. Perhaps very few people have entrée into your personal financial details. Even you. Have you faced your financial soul? Well, now is the time.

First, look at your hands. Your palms. Your fingers. Here's the good news. Those hands, which have consciously taken actions that have worked against you, are the very same hands that will complete the steps that will lead to your new financial life.

When I was a child, money was always an elusive force to me, yet still I knew it was necessary to satisfy my whims. Money brought smiles to the faces of adults and fueled frustration when it was in short supply. Money was a powerful tool whose sole purpose was to leave my possession as quickly as possible and leap into the hands of faceless store clerks. The satisfaction derived from ravenous, unconscious spending was ignited early as I mirrored the behaviors of well-intentioned adults in my life. When I would inquire about a money-related issue out of curiosity, asking "Do I have a bank account?" or "How much does such-and-such cost?" I was told in secretive whispers that the issue was reserved for grown folks.

During my parents' heated arguments, my father often yelled something like, "As hard as I work, you went and bought another dining room set? French provincial? I don't give a damn! Stop spending my money like you crazy!" But my mother knew that my father's tirade would soon subside, just in time for her favorite department store catalogs to arrive in our mailbox. The UPS deliveryman and my mother

Paralyzing Emotions

Emotion	Internal Chatter
Fear	"Money and prosperity are for 'those' families, not ours."
Guilt	"I made bad financial decisions, and I don't trust myself to try again."
Shame	"I have never deserved to be financially secure. I'm just not good enough."
Apathy	"My Supreme Being will make a way. Money is not something my children and I need to deal with."

were on a first-name basis. My mother enjoyed her life as a home-maker, and she made sure her grandiose dreams of being surrounded by luxury became a reality.

My mother cared a great deal that others held our family in high esteem, a far different state of affairs than the struggles she had experienced growing up in Opa-locka, Florida. Raised by a single mother who labored as a domestic, my mother had resented being responsible for her younger siblings during her childhood. She used heading off to college, and later her marriage to my father, as a means to separate herself from her harsh upbringing.

Enamored with soap operas, she was not interested in keeping up with the Joneses; my mother was determined to *be* the Joneses. The life of Duchess, her favorite soap opera character on CBS's *The Young and the Restless*, fueled her determination to be surrounded by a luxurious environment. My mother equated our life living in Europe, at the behest of the US Army, for which my father worked as a career officer, with that of the rich and famous. She took immense glee in sharing with spellbound civilians the tales of our life in Germany and vacations to France, England, and Austria.

My father was the son of a domestic and a sharecropper. He was the eldest of twelve siblings, all raised in rural Georgia. Every child was expected to contribute to the survival of the family, and money was used to satisfy needs. In their childhoods, my parents could only dream of possessing things they wanted. My parents received no childhood lessons about compound interest, investing, or donating. There were no dinnertime conversations about the performance of the stock exchanges, diversifying portfolios, or accumulating assets to transfer wealth to future generations.

My grandparents may have had a coffee can where they gathered the coins and dollar bills that they earned; and as adults my parents eventually opened a savings account, but it was there that their intentional relationships with money ended. Each formed starkly different relationships with money, though not by choice. My father clung to money as a means for his survival. My mother craved money to satisfy the deferred wants that had lurked inside her since she was a young girl.

When my parents met and then married, there came, as with most newlyweds, a collision of affection and financial incompatibility. Their early upbringings had not been a crystal stair, so each brought to the union a relationship with money that had been forged in an uneasy childhood. Growing up in our household, I then formed my own tenuous relationship with money. I adopted from both parents the illusion that the sole purpose of money was to satisfy the wants to which I believed I was entitled and to serve my wants without the requirement that I earn the necessary money. I felt I could squander money because I enjoyed playing the role of financial victim and being rescued by whomever would agree to be my savior.

From time to time, if I received a monetary gift, my parents would suggest that I save a percentage of it. However, that idea would magically disappear whenever a new object would entice me. My father's heart would soften, or my mother would start to think that having another pearl necklace was a great idea. And because my parents would not hold me or themselves financially accountable, I learned how to manipulate cash away from sympathetic adult relatives with a perfectly tuned whine: "If I do my chores, will you give me the money to buy new patent leather boots?" or "If I get good grades, can I get a new toy?" or "All my friends at school have cashmere sweaters and mink gloves—why can't I?"

In my manipulative mind, I knew that my maternal grandmother and her sisters would be my source of an unlimited supply of cash. My grandmother and great-aunts were a gold mine, and they required zero accountability for my spending habits. Whatever I wanted, or even thought about wanting, was promptly purchased during a quick shopping tour of the local mall. Each year, after spending the summer with these gift-giving relatives, I returned home with a brand-new wardrobe, shoes, and accessories. Every item I wanted to have to impress my classmates, my maternal grandmother carefully packed with love into a cardboard box, just in time for the new school year. Throughout the year, my dear grandmother would mail a large box of more clothes, responding to my requests for platform sandals, Big Foot white-fur boots, and *I Dream of Jeannie* plaid corduroy hip-huggers.

The adults in my life became coconspirators in my acquiring every ridiculous fashion trend of the day: day-of-the-week panties, elephant pants, hot pants, jellies, mood rings, and pom-pom socks. And I expected that each year a birthday card would arrive with crisp currency tucked inside, usually a one-hundred-dollar bill, and even a brand-new wallet to carry it in. I never understood the purpose of the wallet; I never had money in one long enough to even rub off the newness. But I saw it as a nice gesture and guessed the wallets had probably been given to my grandmother by the family she worked for.

Instead of cherishing the sentiments inside my holiday and birthday cards, I cared more about whether the envelope was bulky enough to hide a folded hundred-dollar bill or two. Thus I correlated holidays and family celebrations with receiving money. Forget about the sentimental value, shared precious moments with loved ones, and religious observations—from my perspective, these celebrations were for the sole purpose of receiving gifts, which only fostered my entitled attitude. Like their parents, my parents never discussed the income and expenses of the household, talked about investing or making money grow, or taught me tools to save money—nor did I care to learn. All I cared about was that my fleeting wants were fulfilled.

But in the wake of my parent's divorce, the gravy train derailed. Fortunately, my brother and I still had an adoring maternal grandmother and our great-aunts, who doted on us with affection and yummy material goods. I knew that my father left home every morning for a destination called work. He provided the necessary resources for our family to live comfortably around the world, enjoy homes in the United States and Europe, and go on wonderful vacations. He believed in letting "little things" like money be entirely under his domain. As the family breadwinner, my father took his responsibility to provide very seriously, so much so that I never thought that the lifestyle I had become accustomed to would ever change, even upon the divorce of my parents. And my mother, brother, and I did still live comfortably, but my mother had no choice but to enter the workforce. And in the wake of that change, and as a result of the aging of an adoring maternal grandmother and the deaths of my great-aunts, I was forced to realign my indulgent, self-absorbed relationship with money.

Through my adolescent eyes, though my parent's relationship was altered forever, there was still nothing that I should not have. Yet I never knew how money was earned or how it affected my family or my life. Frankly, I really did not care how, in my father's absence, the household was being supported. I never saw a utility bill or a mortgage or bank statement. If I had a bank account, I thought it was my right to make sure that the account maintained a near-zero balance.

Like most teenagers, my childhood friend Vanessa and I learned the latest dances and fantasized about wearing the clothes on the pages of the teenybopper magazines. Vanessa came from a family that included the children in money discussions. She earned an allowance and was encouraged to save her money from babysitting jobs so that she could have money of her own. One summer, Vanessa and I chatted about the new gaucho-style pants that everyone was wearing. We devised a plan to earn the money to buy as many gauchos as our closets could hold. Excitedly, I ran home to ask my mother if I could get a job with Vanessa picking grapes to buy the gaucho pants. "Vanessa's mother said yeah," I reported breathlessly. To my horror, my mother flatly refused. In my mother's mind, only families of lower economic status, unequal to her, allowed their children to work. Not the Lamb family. I was devastated.

That summer, I sat in the picture-framed window in our living room watching Vanessa leave home to pick grapes so that she could earn the money for those beautiful gauchos. She returned home suntanned, with bruised and soiled hands. Still, she was excited to work and earn her own money. And I seethed with envy, even after Vanessa quit five days later after inadvertently walking into a hive full of angry bees. Though she no longer picked grapes, she eventually was hired to babysit for local families. She earned and saved her own money all summer. When we returned to school in the fall, Vanessa wore the latest fashions, but she was most proud of how her bank account had grown. I was enthralled with the money that had enabled her to purchase her own new clothes. In my father's absence, the flow from the money faucet had slowed to a trickle. And because of my mother's frustration with heading a one-parent household, I had to proceed with my financial requests with more caution.

Eventually, as the majority of my classmates secured summer jobs working in various capacities at the Fort Dix military base, my mother finally relented. I was allowed to get a summer job cleaning and serving meals to enlisted personnel at a military cafeteria. When I saw my first paycheck, the spending spree was on. I knew I was rich. Richer than Vanessa, I was sure. Unlike Vanessa, who was required to save portions of her income and contribute to the household, I had no such requirement. I was free to spend my salary as I pleased. Every single nickel was wasted on buying new clothes, Afro puffs, and go-go boots. Not one dime was saved. Not one dollar was placed in a savings account, mutual fund, or college account. And there was zero accountability for my spending.

To show their love during my visits to Miami, my relatives continued to take me shopping, adding to my annual new wardrobe. I could see no need to save my money for a rainy day. There were plenty of adoring people around to make sure I had whatever I desired. And together we all ignored the proverbial elephant in the room: money.

As I reflect on those childhood summers, I now recognize that my maternal grandmother and her siblings were able to be so generous to me because they lived financially responsible lives. They owned their own beautiful homes, had pristine credit, traveled the world, and died completely debt-free. They respected money, knew its power, and understood how it would empower their lives. Their respect was so deep that they would schedule the ends of their vacations to ensure they were home in time to pay their bills! My grandmother and her siblings understood rule number one in the world of money: "It's not how much you earn; it's how much you keep." In my delusion, I thought it was *their* responsibility to properly manage their finances so that they could provide whatever *I* wanted, when I wanted it. It never occurred to me that I should model their financial behavior, nor was it demanded that I do so.

When my dream of being accepted into college came true, I blindly signed the densely written financial aid documents, inserting zeros as assets. I had no appreciation for the fact that student loans required repayment. And who knew the true meaning of late fees, interest, and penalties? Neither my mother nor I understood the ramifications of signing these legal documents.

Soon after I graduated from college, my mother walked into the bedroom I occupied in her home and asked, "What are your plans? What do you want to do with your life?" Although I had applied for graduate school, and she knew that, I gathered her questions had a deeper meaning.

"Well," I answered, "I haven't heard from a few graduate schools or some second job interviews."

My mother placed her hand on her hip and said, "Well, you're going to need to be out of here by next week. I'm not going to have a grown woman living under my roof."

Grown woman? I had just turned twenty-one, but in my mind, I was not a fully realized adult. I behaved like one only from time to time.

My mother continued, "So, you need to decide where you are going to live, because you can't live here."

And there it was. The mother bird kicked the baby bird out of the nest without warning.

Within five days, I chose Atlanta, Georgia, as my destination and boarded an Amtrak night train with one large suitcase and the sixty dollars my mother had given me. Until I found a job as a telephone operator and was able to save enough money for an apartment, I slept in a flea-ridden motel or in the homes of generous new friends.

Thus, without a financial conversation or a financial foundation, I entered adulthood. And I continued to ignore the insistent whispers urging me to save or, at the very least, respect money as a powerful currency, and I lived a flamboyant and fragile financial lifestyle. I blindly abused credit cards, which were aggressively promoted to college and graduate students, ignoring the penalties and how my behavior would affect something called a credit report. I used my flagrant spending to get the attention of my father so that he could ride in and save me . . . until I buried myself yet again. A money issue thumped me on the forehead and asked for a moment of my time, but rather than sit up and pay attention, I chose to ignore it. Credit card purchases were denied, collection agencies called, and apartment rentals were denied. Did I wake up? Heck no! I was too busy getting rid of the Benjamins to care. If money squandering had been an Olympic event, I would have been the undisputed gold medal winner, complete with my photo on a box of Wheaties.

Then I began to notice that lifelong friends had purchased real estate and were funding their retirement funds and investment portfolios. One dear friend, who was a New York City employee, had managed to amass four rental properties over the years and also owned a successful barbershop. Repeating an invitation he had extended on many occasions, he asked me to attend a weekend-long financial seminar at which hundreds of seekers heard the instructors' urgent pleas for us all to get our heads out of the financial sand and get our finances in order. I accepted. That weekend, I asked myself some painful questions:

- ❯ Who got me into my financial mess? *Me.*
- ❯ Who can dig me out of my financial mess? *Me.*
- ❯ What had I been thinking during the majority of my adult life? *I was unconscious.*
- ❯ What mental blocks kept me in a financial graveyard? *The toxic belief that my father or some other individual would ride in on a white horse to rescue me, which would allow me to continue sabotaging my financial condition but fail to take complete responsibility for my actions and my life.*

The whispers of inspiration also asked, "What if children— particularly those who look like me—could receive the financial education I am getting? How different would my life have been had I known how to manage money at an earlier age? How different would my life be if emotional insecurities did not influence the majority of my purchases?"

More important, during that pivotal weekend I asked myself, "How can I influence generations of families by giving their children an early financial blueprint?" I became determined to create an immersive financial experience for others, almost playing catch-up with myself.

And so the children came. Many of these children had never even been taught the most basic introduction to money, nor had their parents. Like my own parents, these parents were not teaching their children anything about money. However, when they learned about the WorldofMoney.org Youth Financial Education Institute, they did not block their child's access for a better life.

No parent or child reading these pages needs to travel this same road. It is my hope that all who read this book will develop the same financial legacy for their children. This book is not about assigning blame or living in monkish austerity. It is about waking up to our money choices and examining how we, as parents and stewards of children, influence their financial choices. Our children become what they see.

■ Speak Your Financial Truth

Before having a conversation with your child, speak your financial truth in an empowering way. I am not referring to shouting in the middle of New York City's Times Square. Instead, acknowledge where you are financially. Speak your truth, without shame, embarrassment, or limitation. Whatever you have known or not known about money has no bearing on your value as a parent or a human being. Before reading one book on disciplined saving, meditate on whether you believe that you and your children are truly worth saving. Of course you do, but how you manage money correlates to what you believe about the beauty in your own life.

Each step a parent takes and each word a parent speaks is a powerful affirmation to reshape the entire family's financial culture. Parents should review the conclusions that they have made about money, which often show up in their vocabularies. Instead of using terms that characterize your current status in a "fixed income," "ain't got," or "poor" sense, use terms reflecting your responsibility and determination to build an empowered life. For example, say, "Instead of purchasing another designer dress, I choose to solidify my financial security." Or rather than articulating, "I don't have any money," assert, "I will have money and will use it to benefit my life and the lives of my children."

■ Rich Delusions

Depending on our pasts, we may pass down our negative financial emotions and behaviors to our children. Because of our upbringings, some of us might feel shame or anger about our present financial status. We may spend money to feed low self-esteem or to try to impress others who could very easily be worse off financially than we are. How we handle our money mirrors how we really value our lives. Many African Americans wear the names of fashion designers on their backs because they do not feel their own existences are valid. Children pick up those signals, internalize those beliefs, and then exhibit the same behaviors.

America is said to be a nation of "haves and have nots." Before we access our bank accounts, we need to examine if we think and behave like haves or like have nots. When these terms are applied to how we think, as opposed to what we possess, we are able to understand more clearly our beliefs about money. Haves move through their lives with self-reliant attitudes. They do not try—they do. Their goals do not depend on external factors. Wealth expresses itself not in the amount of money they earn but in how much they keep and what they believe about it in relation to themselves. Money is exchanged for goods and services, and it is exacting in its response to us depending on how we behave toward it. Whatever we believe about money, so shall it be.

In the African American community, money is often depicted in negative ways. Take, for example, the O'Jays' song "For the Love of Money":

> For the love of money
> People will steal from their mother
> For the love of money
> People will rob their own brother
> For the love of money
> People can't even walk the street

These lyrics can scare you into thinking that the more money you have, the more problems you will attract or that working hard for your money is analogous to the life of a timeworn prostitute. These lyrics focus on the negative instead of all of the opportunities that money can provide, such as the ability to establish charitable foundations that serve others or accumulate financial assets to provide legacies for our children and grandchildren.

Social Security payments and pensions, if they exist, will not be enough to support millions of Americans when they retire. Families need savings plans to survive economic roller coasters, to support the national economy, and to further job creation. With government allocations freezing or being entirely eliminated, parents cannot rely on the benevolence of strangers to provide the cushion their families need. Together with their children, parents need to plan for secure futures and a legacy, no matter what amount is coming in the door. Families that ignore this opportunity do so at their peril.

You may be nodding in agreement right now, but concurring intellectually is the easy part. The challenge and the victory lie in exploring the personality shadows that prevent more black families from moving forward.

In the black community and in society at large, the subject of money is often depicted as negative, bringing with it fleeting emotions—"Mo Money, Mo Problems" by the Notorious B.I.G., "I Got Plenty O' Nuttin'" from George and Ira Gershwin's *Porgy and Bess*. While extreme, the lyrics of these popular songs have left an indelible imprint on those who possess a "have not" consciousness:

Oh, I got plenty o' nuttin'
And nuttin's plenty for me
I got no car, got no mule
I got no misery . . .

The biblical scripture Timothy 6:10 ("The love of money is the root of all evil") is misinterpreted by some members of the black community. Poverty is often worn as a badge of honor and an indication of superiority, and some believe that wrongdoing can be traced to an excessive attachment to material wealth.

Melanie, a single forty-one-year-old office receptionist, despises rich people. These beliefs often pepper her conversations about finances. "Rich people, like Bill Cosby and Oprah, should do a lot more to help the black community. They spend all their money in other countries, but I never see them around my neighborhood." Melanie ignores the fact that Oprah Winfrey and Dr. Bill Cosby's generous contributions to charitable organizations top tens of millions of dollars. In addition to her school for poor girls in South Africa, the Oprah Winfrey Leadership Academy for Girls, Ms. Winfrey has made it possible for more than four hundred black students to receive an education. And these are only some of the philanthropic gestures that are made public; there are countless more. In 1988, Dr. Bill Cosby alone donated $27 million to Spelman College. In Melanie's mind, however, whatever contribution rich people make, they need to do more.

Melanie's negativity toward rich people is actually a diversion. It helps her avoid focusing on the fact that she is four months behind in rent payments and fearful about her own lack of financial security. The end result is that this vulnerable mother passes on a toxic attitude to her three children, who resent financially successful people and wait for an entity or individual to rescue them. Until now, Melanie and her children have never taken the opportunity for self-examination. Like millions of Americans, she cannot point a finger at others and instruct them in how to manage their money when she refuses to do the same for herself.

■ Rich-People Perception Exercise

Parents need to know that neither they nor their children will ever become what they fear or despise. What beliefs do you harbor about those who are financially successful?

During a quiet moment, consider the following statements. Suspend any temptation to write what you believe is the politically correct answer or the right thing to say. Allow yourself to be completely transparent.

Use the space below to write down your feelings about rich people.

When I was a child, I thought rich people were _____

_____

_____

_____

_____

_____ .

My parents believed that rich people were _____

_____

_____

_____

_____

_____ .

Take some time to review your answers.

Next, review the statements below, which are often made concerning rich people. Check the statements you *agree* with. There are no right or wrong answers.

_____ Rich people are stingy.

_____ Rich people are corrupt.

_____ Rich people are spoiled.

_____ Rich people are racist.

_____ Rich people think they are better than everyone else.

_____ The more money you possess, the more problems you have.

_____ Republicans are for the rich.

_____ Democrats look out for the working people.

_____ Rich people should pay more taxes.

_____ Rich people use their money to oppress black people.

_____ When a relative becomes rich or receives a large amount of money, they should help less fortunate family members.

Those who struggle with money in the black community often assume that any well-off or financially secure person sold his soul en route to financial success. In addition, if one has achieved great wealth, it is embarrassing to be called rich. But earning money positively has the power to create tremendous value in the world. People who have financial difficulties might fear changing the circumstances to which they have become accustomed. "The devil you know is better than the devil you don't know," people often say.

Author Marianne Williamson once wrote:

Our deepest fear is not that we are inadequate. Our deepest fear is that we are powerful beyond measure. It is our light, not our darkness, that most frightens us. We ask ourselves, Who am I to be brilliant, gorgeous, talented, fabulous? Actually, who are you not to be? You are a child of God. Your playing small does not serve the world. There is nothing enlightened about shrinking so that other people won't feel insecure around you.

We are all meant to shine, as children do. We were born to make manifest the glory of God that is within us. It's not just in some of us; it's in everyone. And as we let our own light shine, we unconsciously give other people permission to do the same. As we are liberated from our own fear, our presence automatically liberates others.

▪ Self-Inventory

1. What emotions dominate your feelings about money?

    _____

    _____

    _____

2. Do you remember when those emotions first appeared?

    _____

    _____

    _____

3. How did a parent or loved one influence your thoughts about money?

    _____

    _____

    _____

4. What action will you take to change your opinion of money and those who are financially successful?

    _____

    _____

    _____

■ Assignments

- ❯ Tell your financial truth.
- ❯ Release any shame.
- ❯ Honor where you are now.
- ❯ Journal about or record a private video diary of your early money experiences.
- ❯ Acknowledge your financial influences (some examples: family, religion, or popular culture).
- ❯ Identify any paralyzing emotions.
- ❯ Identify any parenting dysfunction in the area of finances.
- ❯ Discuss with your spouse how you can compromise with each other and present a unified front.
- ❯ If you are single parent, where can you compromise and release blocking beliefs?
- ❯ Show your children denominations of money as soon as they can count.
- ❯ Remember, you are not alone.

■ Family Affirmations

- ❯ My family finances are secure.
- ❯ My family enjoys saving more money every day.
- ❯ We are prosperous, healthy, and happy.
- ❯ We spend only what we have.
- ❯ We are building a financially stable future for ourselves.
- ❯ We value ourselves.
- ❯ Our self-worth and net worth are building every day, but our self-worth is not determined by our net worth.
- ❯ We appreciate all that we have.
- ❯ We believe in earning all that we have.
- ❯ We are self-confident, loving, and generous.
- ❯ We live out a positive relationship with money.
- ❯ We respect the power of money.

7

Remaking the Mold

Shana's Story

Shana is a forty-two-year-old single parent. "My son has witnessed that, although I like quality products, I do not and have never lived beyond my means; I have a car that is paid for, I live where I can afford, and I am not an extravagant spender. In addition, I always pay my bills on time (have never been late on a credit card bill and have never bounced a check), I balance my checkbook, and when I cannot afford something, I am sure to explain that we live on a budget and 'it' is not in our budget. On the other hand, my son doesn't observe much of my financial behavior. I have not included him in much of anything to do with my finances. Nor do I make a habit of reading financial periodicals or watching financial shows or news. I'm determined to change this."

NOW WE NEED to help you identify your parental money style. Identifying your parental money style is an empowering process because you will examine your life experiences and relationship with your child from a new perspective. Your personal relationship with money has a direct influence on your parenting style. Identifying your style will also be enlightening, as you may realize that what you wish to express may be at odds with the messages your children are receiving. For example, you may have expressed a Martyr Money Parenting Style instead of a Savvy Money Parenting Style. Instead of believing that you have consistently guided your children as a Savvy Money Parent, you may come to find that you have adopted an Avoidant Money Parenting Style.

The opportunity to adjust your perspective can dramatically shift your family's financial future. If you are like many parents, you grew up without the financial guidance you needed to prepare yourself for your financial future and to discuss finances with your child. You may have operated blindly or mirrored behaviors that became the roadmap for how you would teach your own children about money. As a result, when you are faced with dilemmas in your financial life today, you may find yourself at your wit's end, unsure how to prevent your child from adopting your less-than-stellar habits and attitudes.

Errol, a fifty-one-year-old married police officer, knew that he was unfairly critical and judgmental of his children's impulsive spending habits. After witnessing one of Errol's public tirades, his business partner told him that his attitude not only caused his children to withdraw but could also lead to them rebelling against their own best financial interests.

Your parental money style manifests itself in the emotional intent, power plays, manipulations, and competition that cloud your financial decisions and your interpersonal relationships with your child and other family members. Without an understanding or acknowledgement of your parental money style, you can mistakenly express one motive and achieve a far different outcome than the one you desire. For example, if you operate in the Dictator style, you may misinterpret your child's curiosity or mishandling of finances as insubordination. If you favor the Saboteur style, you may see your child's streak of independence as a threat to your own perpetual need to be rescued.

According to Derrick Watkins, noted author and peak performance expert, parents who struggle with financial matters often unwittingly fall into two categories when it comes to teaching their children about money. "One parent uses their income to provide food, shelter, and clothes for their children and avoids squandering money, while the second parent will use money to control their child's behavior. This parent will purchase $200 sneakers for a moment of peace with their child." Research reveals that there are other powerful parental money styles that merit examination.

■ Identifying Your Parental Money Style

Perhaps you have said, "I will not raise my children the way my parents raised me," or "My parents taught me that money is the root of all evil and I turned out OK, so this approach will work on my children." Or you might excuse yourself by saying, "I don't want my children to think I don't know how to manage money . . . even though I don't. What my child doesn't know won't hurt him."

Have you ever considered how your parental money style affects the messages you send to your children about money? Or, do you improvise your way of teaching your child as a result of your childhood experiences and how you were raised? In many cases, these are defensive responses, not choices founded upon sound child-empowerment principles.

Norma, age forty-six, a publicist and mother of two daughters, said, "One style of parenting does not apply to me. I fluctuate on occasions from being a Dictator to an Avoidant when I can't deal with credit card bills. Honestly, sometimes I wish I lived my life with a victim mentality when I see how my siblings and mom always find a way for others to financially rescue them. Now that I teach my child to become self-reliant and not to model their behavior, I am the black sheep of the family. That is, until they need financial help."

You may not have questioned your parental money style until you were nagged by the feeling that you needed to empower your child with financial education. But your child's expectation that she will get a brand-new car when she gets her license, just like the kids on *My Super Sweet 16*, may have pushed you over the edge. Maybe your desire to keep up with the Joneses is the reason that you spent thousands of dollars on your daughter's spring-break vacation. In either case, you may now be realizing that your current parenting style is no longer effective, but you do not know why. Teaching empowering money skills that are respectful and results-oriented is a challenge that can be easily met. It takes identifying an adaptable, practical parental money style and then making the effort to practice it.

Each style has a basis in entrenched thought patterns, and each action, conscious thought, or subconscious thought has a financial result. No matter your style, each one of us has a "have" or "have not" consciousness. Haves move through their lives with purpose. They do not *want* or *try* anything they do; they make determinations. Their goals do not depend on external factors; instead, haves possess self-reliant attitudes. The chart on the opposite page further dissects the two modes.

■ Parenting Money Styles

"What is within . . . surrounds us." —RAINER MARIA RILKE

Have and have-not thought patterns appear in parental money styles in many different ways. In this chapter, we'll look at the various types and how they impact the lives of children.

Dictator Money Parenting Style

Indicators

- ❯ Secretive and highly demanding but not engaged
- ❯ Attempts to control to an absolute and impossible standard
- ❯ Values obedience and does not allow equal interaction
- ❯ Often doles out harsh punishment

Dictator Money Parent's Message

I fear, therefore I rule and control.

Message to Child

Others must think for you. You are not equal to others. And you will do as I say, not as I do. Your opinion is not valued.

Thought Patterns and Behaviors

Prosperous (Haves)	Lack (Have Nots)
Earn, save, invest, donate.	Earn. Rarely save or invest. Do not donate.
Take full responsibility for their own financial circumstances.	Avoid or take no responsibility for own financial circumstances.
Spend less than they earn.	Spend more than they earn.
Frequently ask, "How can I earn?"	Frequently ask, "Can I have?"
Expect to pay for goods and services.	Actively expect and prefer goods and services that are free (that is, that they don't pay for themselves).
Joyfully pay for goods and services.	Challenge and resent businesses and service providers who charge for their goods and services.
Only earn money positively.	Might earn money negatively.
Use words like "successful" and "prosperous."	Use words like "poor," "free," "hard times," and "don't have."
Donate time and goods to charitable causes.	Rarely donate money, time, and goods to charitable causes.

Darnell's Story

In the wake of his father's death, Darnell, a fifty-eight-year-old maga-zine publisher, consulted with his estate lawyer to make sure his own affairs were in order. His lawyer often encouraged Darnell to inform his wife and two adult sons of the details of the family estate, espe-cially the clause that his wife would be left without financial support in the event of a future marriage after his death, in addition to the fact that his sons would receive one dollar upon his death. Darnell's rationale: "I had to work for everything I have. And I'll be damned if I let some joker live in the house I built after I'm dead. My sons will have to make their way in the world just like I did. And you can forget about some dude living on my sweat with my wife!"

Darnell had provided a comfortable life for his family in their Greenwich, Connecticut, suburb. Yet his wife and sons were pre-vented from knowing the financial intricacies of the family business and were never given access to the financial picture of the business. His wife secretly saved a portion of her monthly allowance, but his sons lived like the money train would never come to an end.

A Dictator Money Parent believes that his duty is to govern his child's financial decisions from birth well into adulthood. Dictator parents do not believe in explaining to their children the mechanics of the world of money, even if they themselves are well versed in personal finance. Dictator parents' primary goal is to maintain control over their lives by disclosing as little information as possible. They focus on what their children do wrong with money, and infractions are pun-ished harshly. The Dictator parent believes children should have little or no money and as little freedom as possible. The subject of money is rarely discussed, except in life-altering circumstances, and these par-ents monitor their children's knowledge of and access to their families' financial information. For example, children may not know if a family will exists or where legal documents are kept. The Dictator Money Par-ent may shelter this information from his or her spouse as well.

Bianca, age fifteen, lives in a tony Washington, DC, suburb with her younger brother and her parents, both of whom are doctors. She attends private schools and spends summers on Martha's Vineyard. Bianca's parents believe that it is not a "child's place" to have a voice in the family's financial affairs. Children of Dictator Money Parents either learn how to circumvent their rigid parents to gain rewards, or they are left vulnerable, forced to handle their own finances without guidance. The Dictator parent may achieve a child's silence, but what occurs in the long run is a child who is not taught how to think for himself with regard to financial decisions, or a child who may inappropriately rebel to exact his independence in reaction to a controlling parent.

The days of "Do what I say without question" are over; this means adopting the attitude that parents and children are equals—not in the sense of life experience or intelligence, but in terms of value. Parents must have clear expectations for their children early on, and they must enforce reasonable limits regarding how money is handled. Children should be given limited choices to help them learn and experience the consequences of their choices and so they can begin to understand that their financial decisions matter. Giving choices balances freedom with responsibility. When children have some control and ownership in their lives, they are more cooperative and have better self-esteem. Parents should balance encouragement and acknowledgment of good financial choices. Intimidation and punishment result in behaviors that bring undesirable consequences, not rewards.

Dictator Money Parents Raise Children Who Are:

- More likely to become financially dependent on others
- Less confident in money management
- More likely to flaunt money
- Not curious about how to manage money
- Likely to appease those they believe are in authority
- More likely to become victims of financial bullies

Ineffectiveness of Dictator Money Parenting

Dictatorial parents generally consider their children's lack of access to how money is managed to be nonnegotiable. Because this style ignores children's perspective and prohibits verbal communication, these children often become passive or rebellious in their relationships. Dictator parents believe that they are always right, and they expect a higher level of maturity than what is normal for their child's age group.

At the same time, a Dictator parent extends her proper authority to the extent of controlling her child as if he were still an infant. This style displays little affection, and the parent's focus on money fulfills only the needs of the parent and disregards the needs of the child. Children of parents with this style become passive and are hesitant to develop their own financial independence. Unfortunately, children raised with this style may experience antisocial peer pressure during adolescence and decide not to share their concerns with their parents, believing they will be ignored or blamed. Further, these children will distance themselves from this style by rebelling against their parents' beliefs about financial management, no matter how correct the information may be.

Release from Being a Dictator Money Parent

A Dictator Money Parent should consider examining what generational legacy they will leave to their children . . . and their descendants. These parents don't purposely seek to sabotage their children's development and ability to have financially stable lives, but sometimes this is the outcome of their parenting style, which can produce children who second-guess themselves with every financial decision. Dictator Money Parents need to remember that negative words and actions do not motivate; instead they hinder their child's development and mindset.

A Dictator Money Parent should remember that his child relies on and adores him. However, this parental money style can unintentionally squander opportunities to develop camaraderie with a child.

Discussing money is the optimal method for forging a healthy alliance, one that is without manipulation, secrecy, or condemnation. While praising and encouraging your child's interest in money matters, have open-ended conversations and avoid judgment. By doing so, you will develop your child into an eager financial team player and build a mutually supportive family.

Eric's story below details how he faced his dictatorial style, stopped condemning his son, and forged a relationship with him based upon trust.

Eric's Story

Eric's twelve-year-old son, Jordan, reluctantly accounted for how he had squandered his allowance money in a matter of hours. Terrified of his father's wrath, Jordan mumbled that he spent the ten dollars on flowers for their new neighbor, thirteen-year-old Tiffany, in an attempt to impress her.

Eric has been trying to open the channels of communication with his son. In the past, he had found that his go-to strategies—lambasting Jordan, telling him how irresponsible and disrespectful of money he was, accusing him of wasting money, refusing to allow him to use his iPhone, and restricting him to his bedroom—did not work.

Eric has decided to use a different strategy to connect with his son. Eric listened to Jordan and heard his son's frustration and feelings of helplessness. Although he would ordinarily have lost his temper, he was touched that his son sought his protection. He decided to try a different approach because he wanted to teach his son to be financially responsible, and at the same time, enhance his self-confidence.

In accounting for his spending, however, Jordan did not mention that he had taken more money from his piggybank without permission, which was a rule at their house. Nor did he mention that he had been lavishly spending his money not only on Tiffany but on other "friends" at school. Jordan loved that everyone at school seemed to want to be his friend, especially when it was time for him to spend his money on them. Jordan remembered how his father had called him "stupid" just last week. As a result, he readied himself for whatever names his father was going to call him now. Jordan was willing to accept the love he was receiving from his peers, even if he had to pay for it.

Eric sat at the dining room table as he listened to Jordan tell him how he had secretly wasted all of his money. To Jordan's surprise, his father did not interrupt or pound his fist on the wooden table. For the first time, his father just listened. Eric remained quiet as his son detailed the candy, ice cream, and doughnuts he had spent his money on. He heard the loneliness and isolation in his son's voice and knew his child was desperately seeking admiration. With compassion, Eric asked Jordan, "Now that your allowance is gone and your piggybank is almost empty, would you rather have the money or the smiles from kids whose names you don't remember?"

Jordan replied, "The money. I would rather have the money. I know they were not trying to be my friends. But I thought maybe if they would get to know me, then they would be my friends." Eric held his tongue before saying anything. In his heart, he had believed that giving his son tough love would enable him to become a financially responsible man. But now he realized that Jordan had used money to receive consolation and friendship and that he was willing to do so, even if he had to deceive his own father. Jordan would rather suffer through being punished and yelled at than forsake a chance at these fleeting friendships.

Eric realized too that if he continued to berate Jordan, his son would distance himself entirely. The next afternoon, Eric surprised Jordan in front of his school. On cue, Jordan's new "friends" excitedly ran over and begged him to buy them treats from the ice cream truck outside. Jordan glanced at his father, then back at his schoolmates, and said, "Not in my budget, fellas, but anytime that you want to treat me, you know where to find me!" On the drive home, Eric praised Jordan. "You handled that situation very well, son. You never have to pay for anyone's friendship. And anytime you want to talk to me about money or anything else, I am here for you."

"Thanks, Dad, I will," Jordan replied, wondering how his father had changed. "And by the way, what's a budget?"

Eric smiled. "Starting this evening, I'll explain."

Empowering Message

Children grow when parents allow them to stumble financially and then start anew.

Martyr Money Parenting Style

Indicators

- Anxious that her child will feel any discomfort, no matter how temporary
- Believes constantly rescuing her child bolsters her role as a parent
- Sacrifices her own needs and personal growth for the desires of her child
- Believes that her child's needs come first

Martyr Money Parent's Message

My life has no value and does not deserve to be financially protected.

Message to Child

Because I believe you can't earn money to stand on your own, I will continue to sacrifice myself. I will always clean up your financial mess.

Belinda's Story

Well-meaning single parent Belinda, age thirty-eight, an executive assistant for a community college, has been exhausted and frustrated ever since her sons Chad and Connor were born. Belinda has denied their school's assessment that both boys have learning disabilities. Instead of investing in tutors and supplemental educational support, Belinda camouflaged her depression over the boys' academic performance by granting her sons' material wishes. When her sons overdrew their checking accounts, Belinda would silently pay their overdraft fees and scold them as they continued to repeat their behavior. Whenever they had skirmishes at school, Belinda refused to make her sons take responsibility; instead, she would reward them by taking them to the local shopping mall to spend money on items she could not afford. According to Belinda, the school authorities were incompetent. Her sons learned that their mother would rescue them from life's inconveniences and that they did not have to respect authority.

Belinda felt it was her duty as a parent to defend and protect her sons against those she believed were attacking them. She refused to allow them to experience the harsh upbringing that she had experienced in a small town in Mississippi. She believed that it was her responsibility to do their homework or badger their teachers into accepting late assignments. She replaced the late-model Nissan she had purchased after one of the boys totaled it (of course, Belinda blamed the other driver). Although she complied when her sons demanded that she immediately purchase another automobile, Belinda, who had developed high blood pressure, was burned out and rightly concerned that her sons were on a very dangerous path. With her retirement account almost depleted, Belinda sought advice.

Martyr Money Parents are financial doormats who have two major beliefs: that they must shield their children from worldly affairs or that they must grant their children's every wish to prevent them from behaving badly. Martyr Money Parents seek their children's permission before requiring that they take on additional responsibility. "John, would you like to learn how to balance a checkbook?" "Mary, do you want to learn how to create a budget?" As a result, because these well-meaning parents prefer to curry their children's favor, they undermine their ability to learn personal finance and other life skills.

How do children become financially responsible adults? By dealing with money and making financial mistakes early in life. For example, if Chad and Connor had overdrawn their checking accounts, Belinda's best choice would be to order them to pay back the bank fees themselves. When Chad and Connor totaled their car, Belinda should have instructed them to get jobs to pay for the damages and save money to pay for a new car—that is, if their behavior and academic performance merited a replacement.

Children don't grow and learn how to manage money unless parents make them accept responsibility for their mistakes. Instead of rushing in to rescue Chad and Connor, Belinda could have raised financially responsible sons by making them solve their own problems. If a child breaks school rules, or especially the law, her parent's responsibility is to help her learn from the experience, not avoid paying the consequences.

The parent's job is to help children respect and budget money so that they can grow to respect their finances. If parents sacrifice their own financial health to satisfy the whims of their children, they encourage the growth of dependent, entitled young adults. For instance, when a Martyr Money Parent perceives his child to be saddled with large debts, often he will rush to the rescue to make his child's experience less stressful. Parents can be financially helpful to their children in some cases, but by and large, the greatest lessons are the ones children learn from personal experience.

Life's demands are great, but the earlier a child develops a self-reliant attitude, the better his chances are of being self-sufficient in the long run. The Martyr Money Parent often tries to shield her child from the pressures of twenty-first century living, up to and including money management. Similarly, when these parents have children who misbehave, they try to eliminate the resultant stressors (like punishment) in their children's world. But remember, the earlier a child becomes responsible for his attitudes and behaviors around money, the more adept he will become at securing his life.

Parents who adopt this style are called martyrs because they are primarily concerned with bonding and showing their love by bestowing material gifts that their children have not earned. The end result of Martyr Money Parenting is that it prevents children from learning from their financial mistakes. The Martyr parent believes that he must prevent his child from experiencing any discomfort in the world of money, and this permissive parenting style results in a codependent child. Parents who adopt this style may have concerns that their children will not like them if they set limits, or they may have experienced a harsh upbringing that they do not want their own children to experience. These parents see themselves as their children's ATM, and they resist their parental responsibility to set limits. They believe their role is to appease the whims and desires of their children and allow freedom with little or no responsibility. As their children become older, these parents may feel that they have no power to alter their children's behavior.

Children without financial limits have no sense of responsibility and have trouble with relationships and honoring boundaries set by others, and they can find the world a difficult place to navigate. Child experts advise that it is unwise to raise children without financial guidelines or to change limits once they have been set. Whether or not they admit it, children do not need or want freedom without financial limitations, but if Martyr Money Parents continue to provide safety nets, many children will not strive for their own independence.

Martyr parents often neglect boundaries, truth, and authority because these things make them feel unloving. Martyr parents interpret resistance from their children as disapproval, which they try hard to avoid. Because a rescuer does not want his children to make mistakes or feel pain, this parent hovers, protects, and saves his child from all financial situations. The Biblical Book of Proverbs shares timeless wisdom on this point: "A hot-tempered man must pay the penalty; if you rescue him, you will have to do it again," and Proverbs 29:21 states, "If a man pampers his servant from youth, he will bring grief in the end."

"I'm his mother, and I will never just leave him out in the cold. If I don't help him, who else will?" sighed Deborah, a fifty-year-old corrections officer. "I take pride in the fact that my son can call on me and I am there to provide." Deborah was not referring to saving her son from a medical emergency. This single mother had just wired her son money for his car payment and a new set of tires.

Deborah neglects contributing to her own retirement fund in order to save her son from the embarrassment of having his late-model truck repossessed. When challenged, Deborah responds, "There is no harm in helping my son every now and then with his rent. No son of my mine is going to be living on the street—not when I have the money to help him. I'm not like a lot of these parents who just let their children fend for themselves. There's nothing wrong with me being there for him."

Deborah does not care to recognize that her son's little emergencies occur on a monthly basis. And, while she recognizes the importance of saving, investing, and donating, Deborah believes that her son will become financially responsible as soon as she finishes paying for his recording studio and the two college courses that he has to repeat after failing them the first time around. The closest Deborah has come to nudging her son toward financial responsibility is cosigning a credit card for him. When he reaches the maximum spending limit, Deborah pays his card balance because she wants to protect his credit more than her own.

Martyr Money Parents Raise Children Who Are:

- More likely to complain about the financial habits of others and not their own
- Embarrassed about their parents' financial affairs
- Likely to learn to lie and manipulate about money

- Likely to avoid taking responsibility for their lives
- Resentful and envious of financially successful people
- More likely to pretend that their lack of financial education is for a higher cause (say, for reasons of religious conviction or a commitment to racial justice)
- More likely to believe that money is used by affluent people to manipulate and oppress others

Ineffectiveness of Martyr Money Parenting

Parents who adopt the Martyr Money Parenting Style teach their children to be helpless and to expect others to solve their financial problems. Children need to develop problem-solving skills to develop healthy relationships with money. Children of Martyr Money Parents learn that the more financial problems they have, the more their parents will rescue them. The sad reality is that these children do not grow up behaviorally, and their learned helplessness carries into adolescence and adulthood.

Martyr Money Parenting is ineffective in that a parent with this style lowers the behavioral expectations for his child. So when the child, for example, blows her allowance or gets into financial trouble, the parent demonstrates that she will be rescued and not have to face the financial consequences of her actions. Children learn that money does not have to be earned and managed—money can be demanded. Further, these children know that, if their parents do not grant their demands, they only need to misbehave in order to get what they want, no matter how badly their demands affect their parents' financial well-being.

The more the Martyr Money Parent protects or condones his child's disrespect for money, the more the child will receive the subliminal message that the parent has no confidence in his abilities. Children of this style receive a clear message: "No matter how much I squander money, my parent will fix it." The parent's logic is, "I am showing my child how much I love her by cleaning up her mistakes." But the child experiences these interactions this way: "My father believes I can't solve my own problems, so that must be true." Children gain self-esteem by overcoming challenges. And Martyr Money Parents should allow their children to experience self-realized victories.

Release from Being a Martyr Money Parent

Martyr Money Parents need to ask themselves, "Am I protecting my child for his sake or to fill my own self-esteem?" In addition, parents with this style should examine their own expectations for and beliefs about their children. For instance, Belinda realized she harbored the belief that her sons did not have the aptitude for money or the ability to be self-reliant. Her own mother had babied her brothers but had been stricter with the girls in the family, and Belinda had been mirroring her mother's belief system in her relationships with Chad and Connor. She explained, "It's a cruel world out there, especially for black boys. I thought I was helping them, but I see I was reinforcing their weaknesses. And I felt if I did not protect them, then no one would."

Parents like Belinda and Deborah need to respect their own preservation, which means they need to make sure their own retirement is secure before satisfying the whims of their children. An enduring, loving relationship with one's child is built upon a foundation of respect. Parents who show their children that they are saving for their own retirement and will not squander their savings to rescue their kids will garner respect—whether or not their children admit it—and will teach an invaluable lesson.

Belinda instituted the following action plan:

- Refusing to reward her children's negative behavior with purchases
- Suspending Chad and Connor's access to their favorite electronics until they consistently earned the privilege
- Requiring positive academic performance while supporting them in this area however necessary

- ❯ Prohibiting them from having a car or playing on their school's basketball team until their grades improved and requiring them to repay the money she spent to compensate the other drivers
- ❯ Holding weekly family finance meetings and having her sons help her research ways to lower household expenses
- ❯ Setting financial limits by creating a budget for her sons' annual school clothes. She said, "No more than this amount will be spent on your clothes. With college applications and tuition only two years away, you two need to begin saving because I have my own retirement to save for."

Deborah understands how she has been spoiling her son; however, she is not able to relinquish her overprotectiveness. Delving deeper, we find that Deborah was raised in a household of three generations of women. Her mother and her grandmother coddled the boys and the men who lived for a short time under their roof. Deborah's female role models taught her that men, instead of providing protection, were to be protected. Though she is not yet taking assertive steps to radically adjust her financial parenting, Deborah is able to admit that she has continued the financial legacy that she witnessed as she was growing up. And that is Deborah's first step.

Leaving a child to struggle through distress may feel like a poor and risky choice for a parent, but parents do well to remember that children do not grow without struggling. I must encourage you to hold back and watch how your children attempt to solve their problems instead of allowing yourself to constantly rush in to make things better. Your parenting instincts, as well as most messages from the popular media, tell you to rush in and protect your child. But if you do that, the message to your child is, "You can't do it," rather than, "You must learn to do it." The message to your child has to be, "You can do it, and I believe that you can."

Empowering Message

You must honor your commitments, financial and otherwise. Be self-reliant and responsible. I believe that you can.

Avoidant Money Parenting Style

Indicators

- ❯ Expects to struggle with money
- ❯ Hides from confronting the reality of family finances
- ❯ Distrustful; refuses to disclose financial matters to family members or consult with a financial advisor
- ❯ Works long hours, but financial documents are disorganized
- ❯ Feels shame and insecurity

Avoidant Money Parent's Message

My finances reflect the chaos in my life. Dealing with my reality is too painful.

Message to Child

You don't deserve money. You are not important. You can't trust people with money. Financial advisors are not to be trusted. Never ask for help. If you don't do things right, you are bad. Never discuss money with your parents. You have to do it all yourself. Money is a distasteful subject. No one cares. Life is hard.

Waymond's Story

Waymond is a married thirty-nine-year-old father of six children.

"I grew up in a working-class section of Houston, Texas, where the only thing more important than breathing was 'looking good.' That is what my father and the older men taught me and my brothers. Although my parents had low-paying jobs, they made sure that we had a brand-new car and enough Christmas presents to fill the toy section of a department store. It did not seem to bother them if the utility or telephone company suspended service. My parents would try their luck down at the dog track. Sometimes they would win; most of the time they would lose. But money was only talked about when you were getting some, losing some, or spending it. I understand how my parents must have felt. It's like talking about money is staring into a dark part of your soul—like it makes you have to face your own reality. Nobody really wants to do that.

"My parents just ignored the subject. Utility bills went unopened; there was no bank account to speak of. In fact, I did not open up a bank account down at the credit union until just before I got married. And that was only because one of their representatives came and made a presentation to my union members. The lady explained that I could avoid paying fees for money orders to pay my bills and that they could also sign me up for direct deposit. I am not willing to go that far and let people all up in my business, knowing how much I make and whatnot. I would rather cash my check so I can count out my money and know that it is all there. That way I can take it home and put it up in the attic in my shoebox, so I can get at it when I want it. Keeping it up there, I don't have anything to worry about it. And my children can't get hold of it. They know nothing about how I handle my money and where I keep it, and it is not for them to know right now. I let my wife handle all of that stuff. When she suggested that we go to a financial advisor, I refused. I don't want anybody looking all through my business. And there are so many scam artists out there claiming to be financial experts, but all they want to do is rip you off. When my wife found out that I didn't pay the tuition for our children's school, she threatened to divorce me. I understand that she was upset, but threatening divorce in front of our kids is no way to handle this. She should know me by now that I won't budge until I am good and ready to."

Avoidant Money Parents engage in behaviors that range from neglecting their finances to rejecting opportunities for their children to learn about money. These parents are not ready to discuss financial issues yesterday, today, or tomorrow. Avoidant parents will delay these conversations until they are confronted with an emergency or backed into a corner. Often feeling a great deal of shame, this type of parent knows what he should do and that his child needs financial education, but he also recognizes that doing so would expose his own mistakes. And this parent will continue to avoid this conversation, possibly for a lifetime.

Donna, age thirty-nine, was a teenage mother and high school dropout. Her daughter, Natalie, is a precocious teenager who possesses a keen interest in saving, investing, and donating money; however, whenever Natalie broaches the subject of the household expenses, Donna deflects the subject because she does not want to be judged by her daughter. When Con Edison or another utility suspends service for lack of payment, Donna feels her daughter is judging her, though she knows in her heart that is not really the case.

Despite her missteps, Donna has managed to nurture a financially responsible child who wants to be a team player at home. "My daughter teaches me all of the things I don't know about money, but sometimes I get tired of explaining why the telephone service is off again," she explains. Donna feels ashamed and believes the unforgiving eyes of the world are upon her, casting judgment on her as a parent.

Derrick Watkins adds, "Parents who let their heart lead them are often the ones whose children avoid learning how to manage money. For these parents, they may feel shame, rejection, and guilt and believe that money is only supposed to make them feel good instead of providing a comfortable lifestyle. These parents are role models for their children to use money only for one's wants as opposed to one's wants and needs."

Raymond's Story

Raymond, a thirty-six-year-old Air Force master sergeant, shares, "I grew up with my parents and brothers in a housing project in Newark, New Jersey. My mother was one of the lunch attendants at my grammar school. Because reputation and status was very important to me, I never wanted anyone to know that my mother was a lunch attendant. My father was a sharp-dressing, good-looking, strong-but-silent type. The only time my parents discussed money was when they argued about my father's disability check. Through beer- and vodka-laced breath, my father used to verbally assault my mother when it came to his money. I thought to myself, 'Boy, that money is a powerful thing.'

"Many of the adults living in my neighborhood owned Cadillacs, the status symbol at the time. They were all living in subsidized housing, but they made sure they had brand-new Cadillacs with loud stereo speakers. People worked hard in my neighborhood so that they could go purchase clothes to make them feel good and then strut and hang out in the parking lot. Whatever you wore had to be not only the latest edition but the most popular brand seen on television and in the magazines.

"In contrast, my father and mother could care less about the brands or who was wearing the latest clothing styles. When Dr. J sneakers were popular, my parents refused to buy them for me. Instead they bought and made me wear plain old Pony sneakers without a logo. After my parents went to work, I drew a red star on the Pony sneakers to resemble Dr. J sneakers and went outside to play basketball. During the game my pants raised up over my Pony sneakers, revealing the fake logo I had drawn. Man, my friends tried to laugh me off the court. My only response was, 'You are wearing expensive sneakers, but I am kicking your butt on this court.' It's not what's on your feet but in your heart.

"As I grew older, I learned that my parent's ability to provide was more important than peer pressure. That is the lesson I hope I am teaching my children today. I'm not perfect, but I am teaching them more than I knew about money at their age. It came a time when my father could not get around like he used to. For the most part he was paralyzed and confined to his bed, yet he still cursed if he could not find his disability check. One day, he called my mother too many names, and she went into their bedroom and slammed the door. All I remember was hearing furniture being moved. I was too frightened to enter the room to see who was getting the worst of all of that noise. After about twenty minutes or so, the bedroom door flew open. My mother walked out like nothing had happened, and from that day on, my father never said an unkind word to my mother again. The lesson I learned? Don't talk to my mother or father about money."

Avoidant Money Parents Raise Children Who Are:

- More likely to become overly financially dependent on others
- Unlikely to feel protected by their parents
- More likely to bribe others for affection
- Not curious about how to manage money
- Likely to appease those they believe are in authority
- More likely to become victims of financial bullies

Ineffectiveness of Avoidant Money Parenting

When children are ignored or not emotionally engaged by Avoidant Money Parents, they will frequently seek external, often negative, pathways to prove their worth. Children are intrigued by money and recognize its power; as a result, many of them will seek to get money by any means necessary. These children receive no financial training at home and have no concept of legal or illegal actions when it comes to acquiring money; thus playing by the rules may not even be a part of their consciousness. Children may come to make fear-based financial decisions and, craving money, may later become aggressive to satisfy their wishes. These children commonly despise rich people because they envy them. They are fixated on what they do not have and lack the ability to appreciate what they do possess. The result is that they become programmed for poverty instead of prosperity.

Release from Being an Avoidant Money Parent

Avoidant Money Parents are often steeped in shame. These parents do not provide their children with the protection and boundaries they need. Parenting of this nature lacks structure, and the financial needs of the children are ignored. Though this parent recognizes the power of money, she chooses to avoid what she believes might be an intimidating relationship. Take Barbara, age fifty-nine, who is raising a teenage granddaughter. She says, "Education on financial responsibility is lacking in our community. When I was growing up, 'prosperity' was not a word used in the African American community. It was all a dream."

Avoidant Money Parents are encouraged to become comfortable in the world of money. These parents can prepare just as if they were planning a visit to a foreign country. For example, they might listen to a language-instruction CD and read books and magazines about the country so that they could become informed and better understand the norms of its society. Applying the same principle to the language and customs of the world of money, Avoidant Money Parents should each spend an hour per day digesting financial media, including radio, television, or newspaper articles, to become fluent with financial terms and culture. The "Recommended Resources" section at the end of the book contains reliable resources for these parents to consider. Increased contact with the subject of personal finance will help Avoidant Money Parents exhibit positive money behaviors for their children and develop self-confidence about building wealth.

Empowering Message

I deserve a healthy relationship with money. I will face my problems head on. I will have healthy conversations about money. I refuse to run from conflict. Money does not exist to make me feel good about myself. My self-worth is deeper than money.

Disneyland Money Parenting Style

- ❯ Wants his child to perceive him in a better financial light than that of "estranged parent"
- ❯ Promotes the child's financial dependency on the parent
- ❯ Teaches her child not to think for herself and not to be financially responsible
- ❯ Teaches financial freedom without financial responsibility
- ❯ Enjoys being his child's ATM

Disneyland Money Parent's Message

Giving money to my child is my value. I will use it to leverage my child's affection and perception of me at all costs. Giving money to my child fills in the gaps of what I did not experience in childhood.

Message to Child

I use money to retaliate against your other parent. You don't have to earn money. I will lavish you with material goods. It is OK to be self-centered.

India's Story

India, a forty-three-year-old single mother of three living in Decatur, Georgia, has grown to resent her former husband Landon's free-for-all parenting; she calls him the Disneyland Daddy. "My children need to learn that money is not free-flowing like it was when their father and I were married. Just because I am learning to be financially responsible does not mean that by doing so I am less of a mother, and I am tired of my ex-husband trying to upstage me."

To provide financially for her children—Alicia (age ten), Rachael (age seven), and Jared (age four), India works two full-time jobs. She is a proofreader and paralegal during the week and takes on additional proofreading projects on weekends. She divorced Landon, a supervisor for a telephone company, three years ago. Now her relationship with Landon is strained at best, hostile at worst. Landon has custody of the children every other weekend and every Monday. India is frustrated that her children love going to their father's home; they tell her, "We can do what we want." Going to their father's house also means a guaranteed visit to the local shopping mall.

Since the divorce, India's children have grown accustomed to having the latest video games and newest PlayStation consoles. Landon also treats the children to concerts and promotional paraphernalia featuring their favorite celebrities. Weekends are filled with shopping sprees, pizza parties for their friends, and the latest movies. At Landon's home, the children do not have any assigned chores—not even homework. Since Monday was granted to Landon in their parent's custody battle, this night becomes, in the minds of the children, part of a long holiday weekend. Their teachers report that the children are behind in their schoolwork and regularly hand in late assignments.

While Landon loves his children, he shares, "After a long day at work, I need to unwind. And I see nothing wrong with my children enjoying being with me. My ex-wife needs to learn not to take life so seriously; perhaps that's why our marriage ended. And honestly, the calculus and stuff they're teaching my kids in school is not something I ever learned. After my day training sales staff, the last thing I am in the mood for is biology. Since India is up on all of that stuff, she can get them up to speed when they stay with her."

When Landon drops the children off at India's modest three-bedroom apartment on Monday evenings, they blabber excitedly about everything their father bought them and all of the money their grandmother gave them. "It is way past their bedtime when I get them settled down. My children are disappointed that they are back home with me, Mean Old Budget-Conscious Mom. My youngest child flat out said, 'You're no fun, Mom. I want to live with my daddy.'"

After the realization sets in for India's children that they are back with her, their exuberance slowly turns into disrespect—especially when India tells them they must deposit the money their father and grandmother gave them into their bank accounts. Her children refuse to account for their expenditures and whine, "Dad doesn't make us do chores!" India says, "While one is talking back, the other acts out, and the middle child just ignores me. And before I know it, Monday nights turn into screaming matches and tears. It is to the point where I don't want to come back to my own home."

The anxiety always spills over into the following morning, when she has to get the kids out of bed for school and get to work on time. In her own words, India's life is "a financial wreck. And my children remind me of that fact daily." India's priorities are to love her children, teach them to be financially responsible, and pay her bills. However, she believes that her financial prudence is causing her to lose control of them at lightning speed. India is at her wit's end, especially when her parenting efforts are undone weekly by her ex-husband.

Landon tries to hide his ineffective parenting skills—as well as his anger and heartbreak over the end of his marriage—by "loving" his children with his deep pockets. He is gratified that his children disrespect India's efforts to rid them of their entitlement attitudes. Landon secretly encourages their rebelliousness because of his negative feelings toward India. Landon gloats when his children brag to India about the material acquisitions he provides. In his words, "India could be driving this new BMW if she had not filed for divorce." Landon uses money as a tool to punish India. And she feels cheated and resentful about the income disparity between her and Landon. She feels that Landon behaves like a child and wants to thwart her efforts to raise empathetic, responsible children.

Many divorced families develop a dynamic in which one parent (often the parent who does not have primary custody) overspends out of guilt or uses bribery to get allegiance or to cover for a lack of effective parenting skills. Separated or divorced parents should not confront one another about these issues, because there is too much unfinished business in these relationships to make taking on an additional dispute a sensible idea. They should, however, discuss with each other how much money is being spent and what it is being spent on.

If you're the parent with less income or financial security, remember two things: First, it is appropriate to explain to your child that you have less money than the other parent. For example, you might say, "I have less money than your daddy because my income has to go further." Second, it is *not* appropriate to resort to name calling, saying, for example, "Daddy's cheap" or "Your mother is a miser."

A parent who attacks the absent parent forces his child to want to defend the other parent, whether verbally or silently. Instead of attacks

or criticisms, you should just say, "I don't have the money." A key strategy to employ when referring to the Disneyland Money Parent is to
provide the necessary information but refrain from negative characterizations. If you realize that *you* are the Disneyland Money Parent,
refrain from making judgmental statements to your child about your
ex-spouse's financial status. Below are examples of conversations you
may have with your child:

Empowering Conversation

CHILD: Does Daddy make more money than you?
PARENT: Yes.
CHILD: Daddy just bought a brand-new boat.
PARENT: That's great! Would you like to learn how you can save for
something that you need or want in the future?

Disempowering Conversation

CHILD: Daddy bought a new motorcycle.
PARENT: There he goes again! He could have used that money for
child support!
CHILD: And we went shopping for a new iPhone.
PARENT: You were saving your money for a rainy day.
CHILD: Daddy says that we enjoy today and let tomorrow take care
of itself.
PARENT: Do you see your Daddy standing here? You're under my roof
and under my rules. Wait until I take care of your no-good
Daddy!

It is far more beneficial for both parents to provide solid financial information rather than negative characterizations. In a separation or divorce situation, when one parent asks the other to reduce
his spending on the kids, the spending parent hears, "You're trying
to take my power away from me." Power is a big issue in separated
and divorced parenting. But if Daddy is indeed buying the child too
many toys, the other parent can make it clear that those toys stay

at Daddy's house. You should expect that there will be some anger about that from both Daddy and the child, but you have to establish these rules, just as you may also have different rules about bedtime: "You go to bed at ten o'clock at Daddy's. You go to bed at nine o'clock here." "You can play with those toys at Daddy's. You can't play with them here." If the child argues with you and asks why he can't have the toys at your home, talk to him when he's calm and explain, "Those toys have to stay at Daddy's because he bought them for you." This will get harder as the child gets older and the money is spent in larger sums, but no matter what, don't make angry comments about your ex to your child. Furthermore, while parents need not feel compelled to negotiate with their child, they also should remain calm in outlining their wishes.

Another critical element of dealing with a Disneyland Money Parent is facing your own emotions. Be honest about your feelings toward your ex-partner. Acknowledge that your ex-partner might currently earn more than you do. If that is the case, you need not believe that your financial status is a reflection on your value or your ability to be a loving and empowering parent. Believing that someone is more valuable based solely upon the amount of one's income negates the humane principle of personal integrity. Conflict often occurs when one parent judges the other parent, who earns less but might be financially responsible and might contribute value to society in ways that aren't tied to money. The parent with a modest salary can still impart a solid financial education to her children.

Children are highly intuitive and can sense the emotional environment in which they reside. Children like Landon and India's are also able to leverage their parent's approach to finances and upset financial lessons to correspond with their desires. The opposing emotions each parent has toward the other's money style also encourage children to rebel, as they do not feel that they live in a household where one tenet is enforced. And the stark reality is that, no matter how much money or material goods one parent throws at a child, these actions will not guarantee children's love.

Estranged parents need to recognize that parenting is a shared lifetime experience. Though they have decided to end their marital relationship, parents should also recognize that the more they are in agreement about their children's financial education, the better equipped their children will be to build a solid financial future. Thus I recommend that parents discuss their unique situations when they are calm and at ease.

When a parent's children return to his custody after spending time with the Disneyland Money Parent, he should allow for transition time during which the children can retreat to their bedrooms or perhaps bathe or do homework. Returning children should not be allowed to brag to their non-Disneyland Money Parent about their shiny new trinkets. More specifically, children should not be allowed to bring chaos into the custodial household; instead they should return to a structured re-entry period.

Disneyland Money Parents Raise Children Who Are:
- Conflicted regarding the Disneyland Parent's use of money
- Delusional regarding the Disneyland Parent's use of money
- Manipulative with estranged parents
- Emotionally unable to handle denial or delay of their wishes
- Burdened with entitlement issues
- Consumed with unhealthy beliefs about their parents' money
- Used as pawns by estranged parents
- Unrealistic about how money is managed
- Taught to believe money should be used to undermine and manipulate

Ineffectiveness of Disneyland Money Parenting

The Disneyland Money Parent is ineffective because she uses money to emotionally focus on her child. Children, being perceptive beings, see that money is a replacement for emotional bonding with their Disneyland Money Parent. These children become conflicted about their own value and the worth of the material possessions that are heaped upon them by this parent. Sadly, these children also often witness a frustrated, financially unstable parent hiding behind false bravado.

Release from Being a Disneyland Money Parent

The Disneyland Money Parent needs to acknowledge the psychological chaos that she creates in the life of her child. Money becomes a third, dominant party in the parent-child relationship. Facing her emotional need to appear financially superior over the other parent is the first step.

Accepting that her child needs her as a parent, and not just the material possessions she provides, is the second step. A child craves time and attention and, to a lesser extent, things. The Disneyland Money Parent needs to know that later in life, when her child recounts his own childhood, he will remember the precious moments they spent together, not the number of shopping bags they accumulated. Before this transformation can occur, however, this parent must accept her own value. All parents, but particularly Disneyland Money Parents, must accept that abiding love for their children is enough.

If a Disneyland parent will not change, the non-Disney parent absolutely must not share his frustrations with or in front of the child. Launching into a fruitless war over who is the better parent must be avoided. Children will seize either opportunity to internalize the toxic emotions between their parents, resulting in feelings of depression, anger, or anxiety. Children could attempt to manipulate the disunity between their parents in order to hurt the noncustodial parent emotionally and appease their own selfish wants. But in the end, even under protest, children respect and prefer structure and consistency. The non-Disney parent should know that his children will flourish as long as his rules are fair, encouraging, and consistent.

Empowering Message

You are enough and, as your parent, so am I.

Saboteur Money Parenting Style

Indicators

- ❯ May receive outside financial support
- ❯ Spends money on valueless products
- ❯ Believes others are responsible for supporting him
- ❯ Unable or unwilling to take action and change her life

Saboteur Money Parent's Message

Prosperity lies outside of me. Victimhood is my power.

Message to Child

You lack the power and intelligence to create your best life. Financial security is for other people.

Erica and Mario's Story

Erica, thirteen, and Mario, nine, cringe when their single mother sends them to the supermarket with her food-stamp debit card to purchase groceries each month. "It seems like we have always been on food stamps. It's like my mother doesn't want to get her GED like she promised so that she can get a better job," shared Erica. "Everybody in our building has been on welfare forever. Not me. I want to graduate from high school, go to college, and be a veterinarian. I want to take care of myself."

Monique's Story

Monique, a twenty-eight-year-old mother of three, is currently pregnant with her fourth child. She lives in Poughkeepsie, New York, and has never been married.

"I want the best for my children. I don't want them to make the same mistakes that I did," Monique shared. "But it seems like every time I take one step forward, something happens with my money, and I have to take three steps backward. I have to start all over again." Financially, Monique has never stood on her own.

For three generations, Monique, her mother, and her grandmother have adopted the Saboteur Money Parenting Money Style and survived on government subsidies. During the brief period when she secured part-time employment, Monique was able to receive disability payments because of the stress she felt during her last pregnancy. Currently, the three women are receiving food stamps and financial subsidies from Social Security and social services; for a time, they received worker's compensation as well. Monique explains, "That nursing attendant training was not for me. And now that I think about it, I think it is better for me to stay home and raise my children. That way I can keep an eye on them and protect them from the gang bangers who live around here. For a while, I thought about going to get my GED, but I am too ashamed."

Monique is aware of how her life could change if she stood up financially and worked to receive her GED. However, she admits that, due to the comfort of knowing that she can be rescued by local, state, and federal agencies, she does not feel compelled to take ownership of her own life. Furthermore, though Monique wears the latest designer clothing and frequently embarks on shopping junkets to upstate New York outlets, she refuses to align her actions with what she knows would be a healthier relationship with money. Monique's childlike perspective about money enables her to justify not earning her GED or using her income to sustain her family. Monique refuses to reap rewards by financially investing in her children's educations and afterschool activities. "Why should I have to pay for my child's karate lesson? There is usually somebody that I can get to pay for it. Why should I get the father of my children to provide for our children? It was my choice to give birth, not his; so it is what it is."

Monique's children attend a renowned charter school that requires no volunteering or financial investment from parents. School officials' underlying expectation is that low-income parents are unable to participate in their children's development. Monique is the perfect example of the Saboteur Money Parenting Style. These parents fear change in their own lives and in the lives of their children. On the surface, this parental type embraces financial education, openly agrees that her children must learn early to save and invest money, and will even meet with a trusted financial advisor to discuss the best college savings plans. But just before the ink dries and the first deposit is to be made, the Saboteur Money Parent experiences a life interruption—say, a sudden illness—and changes or fails to reschedule the appointment with the financial advisor. Though this parent has access to money, she is on a perpetual search for government safety nets to sustain her family. This parent is not willing to volunteer her time, even to the smallest degree, to support organizations that empower her community or her children.

The challenge for this parent's children is that her lack of participation and her expectation of external financial support are passed down to them, making them vulnerable and dependent. This parent does not see her own existence as valuable; she does not recognize her ability to contribute the time, wisdom, and money necessary to put her life on a new trajectory. The Saboteur Money Parent allows some outside entity to thwart her child's efforts to be financially responsible.

The Saboteur also resists taking responsibility for the life she has created. The inner life of the Saboteur Money Parent may be rooted in the belief that her child should not thrive beyond having the basic necessities that the parent received and that the unknown life of comfort and prosperity is to be feared.

The Saboteur Money Parent needs to resist her inner voice and allow small ebbs of change to occur. She needs to allow new financial information to seep into the life of her child and to support her child in the furtherance of that education. When the child of this parent inquires and wants to learn more about money, the Saboteur Money Parent needs to be conscious of the fact that she has been shortchanging herself and her child. The Saboteur Money Parent needs to transform her lethal behavior patterns and not discount her family's ability to process change.

Saboteur Money Parents Raise Children Who Are:

- More likely to feel embarrassed by their parents' handling of money
- More likely to fantasize about having access to material goods
- More likely to equate the absence of money with their personal value
- More likely to resort to negative behavior to receive monetary rewards

Ineffectiveness of Saboteur Money Parenting

A Saboteur Money Parent could argue the benefits of not having to control his life or his financial destiny. This parent may perceive that there is comfort in his lack of knowledge. Unfortunately, this parent fears the unknown and in many cases is threatened by government agencies to maintain minimum access to and use of his finances. This parent was raised in a similar household and rejects any notion of financial self-reliance or advancement.

Release from Being a Saboteur Money Parent

First things first: this parent must acknowledge that his self-doubt is debilitating. Self-inventory is required for a parent to heal his financial saboteur. Transformation will begin, however, once this parent determines that he will increase his self-confidence in small increments. Just like anyone who approaches improving any aspect of his life, this parent may encounter a flood of self-doubt and decide to suspend any financial goals. Giving up all hope, this parent may assume that his family is financially doomed. For most of his life, the Saboteur Money Parent has convinced himself that any positive action for his own and his children's well-being will have a negative outcome.

The Saboteur Money Parent should beware of other people who reinforce this self-doubt, and must instead seek out and maintain relationships with strong financial role models. If you recognize the Saboteur Money Parenting Style in yourself, read the steps you can take to move from self-sabotage to self-renewal on the next page.

❯ Regularly attend adult financial education workshops.

❯ Network and establish friendships with those who are successful in achieving their financial goals.

❯ Avoid at all costs asking yourself, "Why can't I manage my family's money?" Implicit in that question is the belief that "something is wrong with me." Repeating these statements causes your
subconscious to believe what is, in fact, inaccurate and misinter-
prets your life experience and your value as a parent.

❯ Write down your family's financial goal. Describe what you and
your children will feel once you accomplish your goal. Picture
yourself examining your bank statements with a smile on your
face. Decide to pay your bills with joy and appreciation. Visual-
ize yourself donating to those in need.

❯ Write down your negative thoughts about money, and then
change each one into a positive statement. For example, change
"If I save money to purchase a home, my friends will become
jealous, and I don't want to be called a sell-out," to "Change is
good. Home ownership is good. I welcome new friendships with
those who are mutually supportive."

Empowering Message

Because I am learning how to manage our finances, setting financial
goals, and taking action to achieve them, I am showing my child how
to live a financially responsible life.

Freedom Money Parenting Style

Indicators

❯ Tends to be a shopaholic

❯ Passes shopaholic principles on to his children

❯ Refuses to volunteer or contribute financially

❯ Believes a free item is more valuable than a purchased item

Freedom Money Parent's Message

Prosperity is for "those people." I prefer the comfort of being financially taken care of. "Those people" are obligated to provide for me.

Message to Child

Materialism validates me. I am worthless without pretending that I have money to spend.

Mimi's Story

Mimi lives in Toronto, Canada. She is thirty-three years old, the mother of one daughter, and has never married.

"For four generations of my life, I have lived on a financial plantation. My mother and grandmother and great-grandmother were on and continue to be on public assistance. So when I became pregnant with my daughter, I didn't know anything else to do but to sign up for food stamps and public assistance.

"No one expected or taught me to finish high school, go to college, and find a legal way to earn an income. Instead I just copied what everyone around me was doing: collect a government check and go shopping. I was fortunate to move out of my mother's apartment and find subsidized housing on my own. I was always on the lookout for a free this or a free that. Anytime a program charged for something, I did not want to save my money to pay for it. The people operating the programs had made their investments and were having fundraisers, but I never thought to add my two dollars. If it was not free and I could get something for nothing without paying for anything, I got indignant that the people running whatever program had the nerve to charge.

"I appreciate that there are people out here who want to provide education and afterschool programs for me and my children. But what I have noticed is that everybody wants to—or at least the people I grew up with—have their handout and don't want to do anything for themselves to eventually get off public assistance. Nothing wrong with asking for help, but for *generations*?

"I need help. Yes, I do. But what I want is a hand up, not a hand-out. Now that I attended a financial workshop, I am getting my money together and putting a little bit of money aside. I feel like I am part of society. I feel like I am contributing something. And I refuse to teach my daughter the same free poverty mentality. I want to get off this financial plantation where everybody looks at us like we don't have the ability to change our lives. We do. I want my daughter to want more for her life. And more does not come from begging. I guess that starts with me being an example, and I think my daughter is proud of me."

Parents who parent in the Freedom Style *are* stuck on a financial plantation, often for generations. Because their life experiences and their dependent beliefs remain entrenched, these parents do not believe that their lives can be transformed from self-reliance to abundance and opportunity. The Freedom Parent views the world through a prism of scarcity; this parent teaches her children that prosperity and wealth are reserved for other people and not for them. She positions herself to be rescued rather than striving to be a contributor, and as a result, this parent only sees value in free products and services.

The Freedom Money Parent is attracted to using money in ways that only reflect her low self-worth, for example, attempting to satiate her need to "look good"—even as she imperils her family's financial security. In the extreme, this parent may reject guidance to improve her social standing for fear of losing the crutch of free services. The Freedom Money Parenting Style is not reserved for parents from low-income households. Regardless of income, a parent with this consciousness fears independence and does not believe in the power to change her own life.

Freedom Money Parents Raise Children Who Are:

- Less likely to view their parents as authority figures
- Often encouraged to engage in negative financial enterprises

- Susceptible to harboring negative attitudes toward the financially and academically successful
- Lacking the confidence to believe they can positively affect the world
- More likely to believe financially successful people only oppress others
- More likely to believe a financially successful life is reserved for white people
- More likely to reject taking financial responsibility
- More likely to be consumers of predatory businesses such as payday loan and rent-to-own companies
- Seekers of instant gratification and who desire only to satisfy their wants

Ineffectiveness of Freedom Money Parenting

This parental style is closely related to the Saboteur but is far more ingrained. This parent seeks a luxurious lifestyle and the illusion of appearing rich without having to achieve the level of financial education necessary to create such a reality. This parent craves the trappings of success, valuing only materialism, and his child models this behavior. This parent seeks the services and generosity of others, but is reluctant to contribute his own time or dime to sustaining such individuals or institutions.

Release from Being a Freedom Money Parent

This parent should develop relationships with those who are making positive contributions to their communities. Through these individuals, Freedom Parents can see that, as with any other demographic, there are far more compassionate and financially responsible people in their communities than there are dishonest people.

Empowering Message

Together, as a family, we are enough. Let's discover ways to spend time together.

IN SUMMARY, ANY parent associated with a negative Money Parenting Style should not be judged or accused of not loving her child. Every parent does her best to raise her children. However, when it comes to the urgency of a child's financial education, when parents know better, they can choose to live better.

Savvy Money Parenting Style

Indicators

- ❂ Learned financial principles during childhood
- ❂ Passes solid financial principles on to her children
- ❂ Often has multiple streams of income
- ❂ Believes financial education of her children is a duty

Savvy Money Parent's Message

Financial ignorance is a reflection of an impoverished mind. My child has been exposed to great teachings and will use them throughout her entire life. I truly believe that we must leave our children with a morally sound legacy, and being financially knowledgeable is one aspect of this legacy.

Message to Child

I aim to secure your financial education, along with a commitment to academic excellence and community service, so that you and your children may establish a prosperous legacy.

Maritza's Story

Maritza is a married real estate professional and mother of two daughters.

"While we were driving last week, one of my daughters and her friend noticed a rental center. Our daughter explained to her friend that it was best to purchase televisions and furniture versus leasing because of the hidden costs. She explained that the financing would double or triple the original retail price.

"As parents, we have always tried to teach our children the value of responsibility and why it is necessary to learn about the world of money. And we're not just talking about acquiring money—we're talking about giving back to the community."

Dahved's Story

Dahved is a radio personality in both the Caribbean and New York City.

"I am Caribbean and Jewish. From a young age, I remember the lessons my father taught me about money. You don't have to be a rocket scientist or a university graduate to understand the basic concepts of money. Our ancestors understood these concepts and were able to handle more money than we ever did because they were able to save and not spend foolishly. Primarily based around the communal relationships at the synagogue, together our members would save and pool their monies to achieve the goals of the community. For example, we would pool our money to purchase real estate whether or not we had close relationships with one another.

"Through the examples of my elders, I saw the importance of saving, not wasting money, and using it for the greater good. In the same way, I teach my son how to handle money. My son has an allowance and a debit card, so he knows how to handle money and establish credit. Diversification and not betting it all on one horse. He does not know the intricacies of the credit card yet, but he understands that there is a price to be paid for everything, whether it is financially, mentally, or spiritually. I have taught my son the difference between being rich and being wealthy. In our conversations, I explain to him that when you are wealthy, your money is making money hand over fist. Just like parents need to be aware of their child's education, soccer camp, and their child's friends and peers, parents need to make themselves aware of finances. Right now there is no excuse to not know because there is so much information available."

John's Story

John is a senior court clerk who lives in New Jersey with his wife, Grecia, and their four children.

"I was raised by a single mother, and I grew up believing that money was something other people had. When I was in my mid-twenties, I read *Atlas Shrugged* by Ayn Rand, and that has affected my views on money to this day. There is a passage in the book that questions the old adage that the love of money is the root of all evil. It goes on to say that 'Money will not pinch hit for your self-respect' and 'Money will not give you values if you have evaded the knowledge of what to value.' I have tried to pass on these ideas to my children. They are secure in knowing that their needs are always provided for. I have not always made responsible decisions with money, and sometimes that has been a source of family stress.

"My wife, Grecia, and I are the biggest influence on how our children view money. It is not just what we say, but it is everything they see going on in the home. Initially, Grecia and I were not always on the same page, but we discuss an issue and come to a consensus and present a unified front. Many of us walk around with our net worth on our backs or around our necks. We need to relearn a new set of values and reset our priorities when it comes to money and use it to buy things that will endure and hold their value. My wife and I are determined to include our children in part of the conversation when it comes to money. We get into some very serious table talk. We talk openly about the economy, bills, savings, and how our investments are doing. I am still amazed by what they understand and how much they contribute to the conversation. We make plans for our money instead of just spending until it runs out. We are all more aware of how the money gets spent. We have a savings plan and are working with a budget.

"My children see that my wife and I work hard for everything that we have."

Lorne's Story

Fifty-year-old Lorne lives in Queens, New York, with his wife, Phyllis, and their three children.

"If anybody knew how to manage money, my father did. Coming from Grenada, he had sixteen siblings, and he knew poverty. At age eighteen, he moved to Trinidad because he was determined to make a successful life for himself. And he never lived beyond his financial means. My father never hung his hat where his hands could not reach. He also taught me to save for a rainy day. After our family moved to America, [when I was] fourteen, my father opened a bank and a Christmas Club account for me. He was the driving force behind managing my deposits from my allowance and from my summer job. He did not know about investment products, but he definitely knew how to save. He saved enough cash for a down payment for our house. On the day my father passed away, he was debt-free.

"The difference with my father in teaching my children is that I have a little more knowledge in teaching my children. And even though I was stubborn about discussing our family matters with my children, I now see that silence does not empower them. My wife and I have regular family financial discussions with our children, and I continue to be amazed at how aware they are."

During President Obama's 2012 White House Summit on Financial Capability and Empowerment, an audience of national thought leaders dedicated to providing financial education in their respective cities listened as young people expressed appreciation for the personal finance courses in their schools. One young man, standing confidently behind the podium, said, "I was a foster child since I was eight years old. I lived in a troubled neighborhood, but inside I knew that I had to work hard to have more in my life. It was not until I took a business and personal finance course in high school that I knew I could have a stable life. In a few months, I will graduate from college with a degree in business. And in the fall, I will attend Yale Business School. To everyone [hearing] the sound of my voice, please continue to teach young people how to use money so that they can have the great life I am going to have as a financially secure businessman."

In a perfect world, every parent would have been taught during childhood about the impact of money on their lives. Not every parent had that experience growing up, but as adults they can become savvy and increase their financial knowledge along with their children. Every parent can become savvy by openly discussing the subject of money and regularly reading and viewing financial media with their children.

A Savvy Money Parent is willing to set aside her desire to be a fantasy hero for her children. Instead, she honestly faces her fears and frustrations while learning at the same time.

Savvy Money Parents Raise Children Who Are:

- Confident
- More likely to base their thinking and actions on reality
- Independent
- Financial team players
- Strategists
- Cogent thinkers
- Ambitious
- Service-oriented and generous

Empowering Message

I see no benefit in encouraging your dependence on me. Instead, I see your ability to create a life that is more than I ever dreamed of. My expectations for you are higher than the highest mountain because I know you can achieve great things by leading a self-reliant and financially responsible life.

■ Financial Parenting for Couples

Carla's Story

Because of her stately, kind demeanor, one might be surprised to discover how heavily financial pressures weigh on forty-year-old Carla. "The biggest influence on my child's attitude toward money is from me and my husband, Mitchell. She sees us arguing about money, and more importantly, she knows we have different beliefs about how we should wisely use money for our family. She uses our disunity to get what she wants."

Parents with incompatible Money Parenting Styles can still work together to positively educate their children. Secretly going behind a spouse's back, rather than attempting to collaborate, will undermine the marriage. Quite simply, parents have to minimize each other's weaknesses, maximize each other's strengths, and find a middle ground in their styles that works in a positive way. For example, if one parent is extremely frugal and fearful of spending money and the other parent is much more brave and willing to take risks with investments, then they should find a middle ground that actually works for their family's culture of finance.

The outcomes for a child whose parents work against one another are varied. That child may become very conflicted about money and come to see it as something that causes strife and unhappiness. Even worse, she may begin to have a very selfish and singular view of money, believing that she must always work alone and protect her own interests. A child can even become financially responsible when she has financially irresponsible parents if the child uses her parents as an example of which behaviors not to model. But most often these children will imitate their parents and will also be financially irresponsible—until life intercedes with glaring lessons or trusted advisors intervene to guide them appropriately.

Constance and Ron's Story

Constance, age thirty-five, is a married mother of one and is currently pregnant with twins. She admits that her husband, Ron, keeps both her and their daughter on a tight financial leash. "I've tried to discuss his complete disregard and lack of compassion for my feelings and the kind of life I wish to live. My husband rarely praises our daughter, Sara, who does well in school and never disobeys our wishes. But frankly, I'm tired of living under his thumb, asking for permission to spend one dime or to have access to our financial situation. When I broach the subject, Ron argues and questions my support of him. Yet when he asks for an itemized statement of my monthly expenditures, I always comply. When I wanted to open a bank account for my daughter, Ron refused. Perhaps it is in response to Ron refusing to talk with [Sara] about money, but when she innocently asked how much money he made, I thought he would have a heart attack. Ron scolded our daughter and told her that the subject of money was grown folks' business. Sara is beginning to take her frustration out on me because she is afraid of her father."

Constance further shared that her marriage was a replay of her childhood. Like her own daughter, she had craved her father's approval and tried to fit into society's definition of a "good girl." She knew that, when she married and had her own children, she didn't want her children to be excluded from a basic financial education the way that she had been. Her father had hidden that he was not paying the household bills; utilities such as the telephone and the electricity were constantly being shut off. Seeing her family's belongings being removed by the sheriff is a bad dream that she constantly replays. Constance now wants each member of her own family to be considered a valued part of the team.

Ron has a different perspective: "I have never been the affectionate type of person. I show my love by providing for my family and making sure that they have a nice home to live in. I've heard Constance's complaints before, but what she fails to admit is that she is a poor money manager. Plus, I can't really trust my wife. Imagine how I felt when I found out Constance had a secret bank account. How do you think I felt when my wife went out and bought a toy for my child—a toy that I told my wife and child was not in the budget? If I was to allow her to handle our family's financial matters, I fear that she would make a total mess of things. I'm not trying to buy my children's love with money. They are children, not my equal partners. When my children reach maturity, I will assess their ability to understand money. Until then, my children should focus on being children, and my wife needs to focus on being a good wife."

Constance and Ron are clear examples of the Martyr and Dictator Money Parenting Styles. The consequences of both styles are that their children either will not value themselves or will have severe conflicting entitlement issues and will manipulate one parent in order to pit him or her against the other.

Neither money style is an effective method of nurturing self-reliant and financially responsible children. Parents should not attempt to acquiesce to every want of their children, nor should they control their children by withholding crucial information about how the world of money operates. A child's curiosity about the world of money is a positive indication of his desire to participate in the world. Dictator parents tend to violate their children with toxic emotions; Martyr parents are unwilling to set solid limits on unacceptable behavior.

Parents must applaud and reward their children's curiosity about the world of money by explaining the simple mechanics of money and enforcing a solid value system of philanthropy and service to the world. At the same time, parents like Constance and Ron should do their own emotional inner work so that they do not spend their lives acting out painful episodes from their childhoods in front of their children. Ron's desire to dominate financially and Constance's desire to be permissive financially are reflections of their own wounded inner children. The two should consider that they are expressing their insecurities about their own self-worth by refusing to engage with money in a positive manner.

Children of parents with conflicting money styles tend to live fearfully and tentatively, and more often than not, they lack the ability to make their own financial decisions.

Gigi's Story

Gigi, age thirty-nine, is a bank vice president and the mother of three daughters in New Jersey. "Growing up Muslim and first-generation Egyptian American, [I watched as] my female family members worked and gave their paychecks to the men in their lives. My mother had a successful salon and was a great businesswoman, but when she came home she handed over her money to my father. Then women were relegated to household duties and raising the children. I saw the female figures with their hand always out to men to purchase household items or asking for money to buy whatever they needed.

"At sixteen years of age, I decided that I was not going to live like that. My mother and I frequently butted heads when I questioned her behavior. She would answer, 'Being financially independent is not how the world works.' I replied, 'You're going to have to give me a better answer than that.' In spite of my father's conservative views on the roles of women, I preferred to be next to my father balancing the checkbook. He didn't know this, but I was feeding off of the masculine ways of running a household. While my father balanced the checkbook and monitored the family budget and doled out money to my mother, he didn't notice that I sat nearby taking it all in. I recognized at a young age that the power [lay] in controlling the household money.

"The only problem is that I married a man who is just like my mother. He does not realize that love does not pay the rent. My husband does not care how his carelessness affects our family. Now my daughters witness their father and I bickering about money. My husband does not believe the tenets in the Holy Koran apply to him, even though the imam at the mosque strictly states that the husband must provide for his family. The wife does not have to work if she does not want to, but that means that the husband must earn sufficient wages to support the household.

"Now that we are separated, I teach my daughters that growth and change is always good to kick us out of our comfort zone. I also founded an organization dedicated to breaking cultural stigmas for women who do not have a say in their financial lives. Now I am determined to be a role model for my daughters and show them that there is no taboo to managing and saving your own money. Gone are the days that a woman has to hand her money over to a man. I teach my daughters to pay for themselves first. I want to show my daughters not to give up financial control over their lives.

"I could handle my husband's disruptive behavior, but the most stressful time as a parent is when my husband and I don't agree on how to handle our children's behavior. When my husband and I don't agree, the whole system shuts down."

It is very stressful and counterproductive when parents do not agree on how to address their children's financial education, but disagreement is to be expected. There are many reasons parents disagree on how to manage their money. Perhaps they grew up under different parenting styles. His parents handled behavior one way, but in the home where she grew up, discipline was handled very differently. Each parent has a different temperament with different behavioral expectations.

Believe it or not, though overcoming these disagreements is a challenge, experiencing this conflict doesn't mean that parenting in the home is doomed to fail. Parents with differing approaches should take the opportunity to blend their respective approaches for the long-term benefit of their children. Dysfunctional financial parents do themselves and their children a disservice by working against one another to achieve the same goal. The following are the most common dysfunctional types:

- **The Abdicator Parent:** If not acknowledged and corrected, abdicating one's parental obligation in teaching a child about money can cause great disruption in the family. Often, out of frustration or helplessness, one parent will abdicate their parenting role by turning that responsibility over to the other parent. Placing one parent in the position of being the enforcer—and ensuring that she is seen by the child as the financial decision maker—leaves the abdicating parent in a passive role. Alternatively, should the less assertive parent include his spouse in creating a unified financial code, the child may devise her own understanding of the world of money and manipulate her parents for her own wishes. Parents who prefer abdication over engagement may feel that giving up responsibility is easier than arguing. Mantra: "I am fed up with talking about money. You deal with it!"

- **The Saboteur Parent:** Another dysfunctional approach to differing parental opinions is sabotage. One parent attempts to subvert the other parent—but does so only in private. "Don't worry about what your dad said. I'll buy it for you later when he's not around." This tactic teaches children to withhold trust and that their parents are to be divided and then conquered. Financial goal setting and frank discussions about money are not aspects of the parent-child relationship or the parents' marriage. Mantra: "My financial actions will be our little secret."

- **The Dominator Parent:** Children witnessing a marriage with a Dominator Parent are taught that money is used to wield control over the other spouse. A child may side with the more or less powerful parent, depending on his own personality, thus causing an emotional imbalance in the home. Mantra: "When it comes to how money will be handled, it's my way or the highway."

Unified Financial Couples

For the sake of the children and long-term family prosperity and harmony, parents need to examine and embrace their different approaches to money and show a unified front. Spouses need to first understand each other's experiences with money and then reach a consensus on how to empower their children.

When parents encounter an area of disagreement, they should meet—separately from the children—to discuss their opinions and decide what decision would benefit the long-term financial goals of the family. Together, both parents should devise a financial plan and approach that they are willing to support. In many homes one parent serves as the disciplinarian/bad cop while the other parent acts as the relationship nurturer/good cop. Knowing the other's weaknesses, each parent can support his or her spouse in financial issues so that their children cannot have their desires appeased with a divide-and-conquer strategy.

As a result of a unified approach, each child will come to understand that the family must operate as a business in order for the unit to prosper. The children will receive the structure they need while still being taught financial responsibility. In a single-parent home, this approach still applies, as a parent will need to embrace his or her need to emotionally appease the children, while at the same time giving them the tools to become self-reliant. When parents refuse or are unable to work together to teach their children money management, or when they do not respect each other's perspectives and decisions, everyone loses. Whether in a two-parent home or a situation in which the parents don't live under the same roof, parents should decide to be responsible and unified role models.

■ Moving Forward

No matter what Parenting Money Styles parents may presently have, they can empower themselves by embracing three concepts: expectations, just rewards, and accountability. Working with their children to understand and live under these financial guidelines will help them to become Savvy Money Parents and help their children to become savvy adults.

Expectation

Beginning with themselves, parents need to expect that both parents and the children adhere to the rules of the family's financial plan. By releasing any notion that access to financial resources makes one a better parent, a parent can calmly state to her child, "Daddy and I both love you, and you will abide by our rules when it comes to saving and budgeting. These are our expectations." Parent must refuse to debate or argue this point. In fact, a parent should state her expectations (for example, telling her child to do a chore) and then walk away. You must never leave an opening for your child to believe that there is room to debate about the boundaries you have set.

Just Rewards

One of the most debilitating parental roles is the Santa Claus paradigm. In the Santa Claus style of parenting, parents often purchase items in response to their children's demands in order to get their children to behave in a particular manner. But there is an important distinction between purchasing items to reward your children's positive behavior and purchasing items in order to get your children to behave. For example, when a parent purchases a brand-new Kindle for her child because he performed volunteer work in the neighborhood, that is a just reward, especially if the parent does not do so in exchange for, or on each occasion of, their child's service. A parent's promise to buy a teenager an iPhone for cleaning his bedroom is a Santa Claus bribe. When you purchase concert tickets for your son after he makes you feel guilty for being divorced, or when you don't require your adult daughter to contribute financially to the household because you are afraid she will not allow you to see your grandson, that is Santa Claus parenting. Just-rewards parenting enables children to develop healthy self-esteem by improving their circumstances. But dangling a reward in front of children for doing what they should do on their own feeds into a dangerous entitlement syndrome, whereby children believe that they deserve to be rewarded without earning the benefit.

Accountability

It's time to hit the reset button on your accountability to your child. Each parent is challenged to work in accord with his co-parent. Each parent is challenged to bring his child into the family unit with a healthy discussion of the family's money.

Should either parent lack the tools to do this alone, the two should consider asking a trusted family advisor or friend to lead the discussion. No matter whose custody the child may be in, both parents need to participate in examining and adjusting their behaviors and attitudes about money. For example, if a child attempts to manipulate his mother through guilt because she may have less financial resources, the father should not endorse the child's behavior. The father or other parental figure should step in and support the custodial parent.

As an example, consider how Danielle's parents in the scenario below could handle her accusations that her mother is ruining her life because she makes her account for how she spends her allowance.

Empowering Conversation

DANIELLE: Daddy lets me spend my money how I want to!

MOTHER: You will not learn how to save and budget your money if you don't start practicing those skills now.

FATHER: Danielle, though I struggled with money in my life, I am trying to be more responsible. In any case, you will respect your mother and honor her wishes.

When it comes to money, parents must learn, as in any other area of their children's lives, how and when to set boundaries. Parents must decide in advance when money is to be utilized and the amount to be spent. Both parents must recognize that conflict surrounding incompatible parental styles is often a symptom of the chaos in the marriage. In the case of a single parent, miscommunication is a reflection of discord within the parent. Never use money to drive a wedge between your child and your co-parent. And don't use money to demonstrate your worth as a parent. Doing so will absolutely backfire on you.

Coming to terms with your money style and taking the necessary steps to align your emotions and long-held attitudes about money will shift your relationship with yourself and your child in a powerful way. Your open discovery of this issue will transform your life so that you and your child can be active participants in the world, absent the controls and toxicity that we often teach our children when we don't know better.

Your child awaits this discussion. Your child will welcome your transformation. Using money to teach dependence, love, allegiance, silence, or control is only a transitory bandage that will cause manipulation and false entitlement and encourage your child to adopt a financial fantasy. Your child should know that you are not Warren Buffett or Oprah Winfrey. Will your child still respect and still love you? Absolutely, yes. Your child loves you now, warts and all.

▪ Assignments

- Identify which parenting money style resonates with you.
- Journal your personal reflections.
- Discuss your reflections with your spouse or other family member and then share your thoughts with your child.
- Elicit your spouse's and children's ideas about how your family can adopt healthy financial behaviors.

8

Growing the Family Estate

DISCARD THE NOTION that discussing the subject of money with your children is taboo. Let go of the idea that you must to appear to be superhuman to your child. Conduct a self-inventory of toxic attitudes you might possess about money. Then acknowledge and release them.

Schedule a family meeting and calmly explain to your child that your family is akin to a business. And, like any business, everyone in the household is responsible for accumulating assets and monitoring monthly expenditures. Show your child all of the bills for the household, what you owe, and what your income and credit scores are.

Once they believe they can contribute to the household, children will no longer behave as though your money grows on trees. Your child will become highly engaged in the management of the household finances. And because they are competitive and have a love for money, children will like brainstorming ideas to retain money rather than squander it. But your child's shift in consciousness must begin with you.

During your family meeting, move beyond only showing financial documents. Also share what you learned from your own parents about money, either through their instruction or from your observations of their behavior. Share with your child the financial fears you had as a child. What do you wish you knew more about regarding money? What were the positive and negative aspects of your family's financial culture? How did your religion or spiritual path inform your understanding of the world of money?

Schedule weekly or twice-monthly family money meetings to make sure you are meeting your saving goals and to set new priorities. Ask for your children's input on how your family unit can begin to save more money. Exude an easygoing manner and avoid conveying any severe anxiety you may be feeling without discussing the source of your frustration.

It is important that your child actually see the costs of running your household. Children are resilient, competitive, and creative. They have a high regard for fairness and hate injustice. If they feel cheated or lied to regarding money, it will be difficult to regain their trust.

Melody's Story

Melody, age thirty-two, is a single mother. "I was hesitant to tell my daughter about the anger I held toward her grandfather—how I wished he had supported our family and didn't desert us, leaving my mother with the responsibility of raising five children alone. But as I candidly told my daughter my history with money and how I wanted a better life for her, she softly held my hand and said, 'Mommy, don't worry. I know I waste my money and that you worry about me. But I am determined and I think that together we can do this.'"

■ Monitor Your Words

Parents who lie about money teach their children to do the same. The parents may not explicitly tell their children to lie, but children see how parents may avoid paying bills by disguising their voices or claiming not to be home when the collection agency calls, for example. As children mirror the big and little lies of their parents, they become more comfortable with being deceptive. And the more children see you lie, the more they will lie themselves. Thus, if a parent claims to be broke and his child sees currency in his wallet, the child may later lie about her allowance and expenditures, among other things. Furthermore, the child may lose trust in the parent.

Children often see their experiences through absolutes. They witness, through their parent's expressed conflict and open frustration, that money generates conflict and discomfort. Therefore, they find that dishonesty is an easy way to avoid arguments. So when the parent says, "I told you not to waste your allowance on lip gloss," the child may feel this is the perfect white-lie scenario: she can make her father feel better by telling him the lip gloss was a gift from a friend. Faced with continuous lies, parents will learn less and less about the lives of their children.

As in all facets of their relationships, children must feel that parents will welcome discussions about money without judgment. The parents who are consistent in engaging and guiding children along a path to financial responsibility can establish expectations and goals while supporting their children's autonomy, allowing them the freedom to make their own decisions.

The language you use about money can have a powerful impact on your children's well-being and their relationships with money. Changing the words you use to characterize money can eliminate fear about your financial status, promote honest communication, and direct your children toward independence. The words we use to discuss our finances not only reflect our own feelings but also affect our children's feelings.

You can create the energy to transform your own relationship with money by knowing what to say to yourself and to your children. For example, Adam, a married, forty-six-year-old New York City fire captain, would always respond to his son's requests for money by saying, "I'm flat broke. I ain't got no money." His son, Aaron, age twelve, would always protest, causing friction in their relationship; he believed that his father was being dishonest with him. He would witness his parents planning one of their gambling junkets to Atlantic City and say, "I just saw you pay for your gambling trip! Plus there is money in your wallet."

Adam, who had a Dictator Money Parenting Style, believed that his son was being disrespectful by questioning his response. "Aaron is a child. I don't owe any child an explanation on how I spend my money." While that may be partially true, children know when they are being overtly misled, and this leads to distrust. It is imperative that parents discard words that do not serve them and that perpetuate victimhood, which is then passed on to their children.

The lists below show how parents can upgrade their vocabularies to begin removing the vestiges of victimhood from their words. Being honest with your children about financial matters is freeing. In opening up to others about your financial reality, you also open up in such a way that you are more accountable to *yourself*. In the power of words lies the ability to create a cohesive family culture, one in which parents and children no longer need to pretend to be heroic figures.

Ineffective Approach

- "You must think money grows on trees!"
- "I'm broke."
- "Do you want everything you see? You don't appreciate anything!"

Empowering Approach

- "Your mother and I have decided that isn't in our budget this month."
- "How could our family earn extra money for that item?"
- "Add that product to your list, and then each month you can choose which item you want to purchase with your allowance."

Make every attempt to eliminate these limiting words:

- Fixed Income: Declaring that one is on a "fixed income" indicates that a parent intends for this status to be permanent. Instead say, "Currently, my income is less than I would like it to be, but I am determined to create a solid financial foundation for our family."

- Poor/Broke: Instead of referring to oneself as "poor" or "broke," say, "I have money, but I need to use it more wisely."
- Free: Instead of putting undue value on free products and services, say, "I value opportunities through which I can support trusted businesses and service providers with my money."
- No Income: This one is popular when a parent suddenly loses his or her job. Say, "We are fortunate to have each other to protect and love, and I am excited about the next chapter in my career."

■ Why Parents Lie to Their Children About Money

Protection

The most common reason parents lie to children about money is a desire to protect them. Parents want to shield their children from the evils of world. While understandable, when this impulse is taken too far, children will be confronted in a harsh way with how money impacts their lives. Parents, in protecting their children, want to preserve their innocence, and they adore seeing their children's helplessness. Ellen, age twenty-eight, was taught as a child that "young women need to rely on their husbands to provide for them." Of course, there are age-appropriate discussions surrounding money that require a certain amount of discretion; however, in most cases, honesty is the best policy.

Ego

Parents who focus on their power position may not initiate discussions about money. This parent might believe their children rank below them and do not merit these types of conversations. Alternatively, parents may want to maintain the illusion that they are their children's eternal heroes. Discuss financial matters may expose these parents' own fragile finances and cause their carefully constructed facade to crumble.

Frustration and Peace

Parents tend to lie to their children about money out of a momentary inability to communicate and a desire to have peace. After a hard day at work, no parent wants to be confronted by a whining child and have a protracted conversation about money. Often a parent will lie just to shut little Timmy up.

Parents should keep in mind that their children will lie to them for the very same reason. Thus, no matter the reason, when your child comes to you to talk about money, a constructive response is warranted. For example, if he asks for your money to make a purchase, ask him, "How do you propose to earn the money for the sneakers so that you can pay for them with your own money?" Or you could simply tell him, "A $100 pair of sneakers is not in my budget this month." If you want to build up your child's knowledge about comparison shopping, tell him to find the lowest price for those sneakers. Once he has done so, visit http://finance.yahoo.com and www.nasdaq.com and determine the stock price of the company that produces them. In addition, you could ask, "Have you made a deposit in your mutual fund to buy stock in that sneaker company?" After that, he must choose a charity to which he can donate some of his other sneakers and clothes.

■ Honesty Is the Best Policy

Honesty is an important quality in a relationship between a parent and a child. Our children are resilient and want to be told the unbiased truth. Being naturally intuitive, children know when they are being misled. Benjamin remembers, "It took years for me to understand why my mother would give her modest earnings to the church when my brothers and I barely had enough to eat. I know now that my mother had a misguided understanding about personal finance that did not turn around until my uncle started advising the family. Then I witnessed my mother taking control of her life instead of blindly giving away all of her earnings."

When you are unsure about something, the best and most honest answer you can give your child is, "I don't know, but let's find the answer together." Parents need the trust and respect of their children if they are to lead them. Milton, age eighteen, shares, "I love my mother, but I can't trust her. Ever since she withdrew my money from my bank account to pay for her boyfriend's new car, I can't let her get too close to me. When I complained, she blamed me, as if I had no right to say what was done with the money I earned on my part-time jobs."

Children also want an open line of communication. They need to know that you are teaching them about money without bias or your own emotional baggage. Disengaged parents will raise disengaged children. Financially hypocritical parents will raise another generation of hypocrites. Alternatively, parents who set out to ingrain good financial habits in their children and guide them toward academic excellence and community service will see their children blossom into responsible and productive adults.

■ Assignments

Journal your responses to the following questions:

- ❯ When, if ever, did your parents lie to you about money?
- ❯ When, if ever, have you been dishonest with your children about money?
- ❯ Why were you dishonest? How did your child respond?
- ❯ How can you be honest with your child while maintaining your desired degree of privacy?

9

Seizing Control

"The surest way to ruin a man who does not know how to handle money is to give him more." —George Bernard Shaw

WANT TO CREATE an unproductive adult? Allow your children to develop a false sense of entitlement. A child is entitled to be treated lovingly and respectfully by his parents and to have his needs met—food, shelter, and items the family can afford. Children are not entitled to $250 pairs of sneakers or brand-new Maybach automobiles, but some parents unknowingly promote this false sense of entitlement from birth. Then, when their children begin to make demands, parents do not know how to seize control.

Children who do not develop a healthy respect for money learn to think this way: "I don't have to earn anything. There's a reward for manipulating my parents, and I'm entitled to all the things I want." Instant gratification is a mindset passed from adults to young people.

Today, many children and adults believe that they need not work for anything and that the money gods will bestow millions upon them. In every generation, young people aspire to be rich. Period. When they are questioned further about this, youth will share that they want to emulate their favorite entertainers—rappers, athletes, and superstars.

However, when young people are asked to share how they are going to execute their plans to become rich, they have no idea where they would begin. The instant gratification mindset leads them to believe that without a work ethic they need only wish to be millionaires, and that they need not work or learn to manage money properly.

Seizing control of your financial behavior and conversations with your child about money will become a defining moment in your life. This process also includes understanding what life and educational expectations your child has for himself. The *Chronicle of Higher Education*, in an article titled "Redefining Admissions 'Success' for Black Males," reports that children from communities of color often lack ambition when it comes to charting their college careers. More often than not, this decision, whether deciding to attend an Ivy League university or the local community college, reflects your child's self-worth. One's willingness to be financially responsible or prosperous hinges on one's self-worth. Many WorldofMoney.org Youth Financial Education Institute students reported, "Before I felt better about my abilities, I did not believe that I deserved to have money, so I wasted it."

By developing a strategic plan, you will propel your child toward establishing security and prosperity in her life. Now, as we discussed in earlier chapters, you will no longer ignore the elephant in the room when you establish an action plan. Like most children, your child probably believes that she is immortal and that the day will never arrive when she needs a retirement fund or experiences an emergency. However, you know otherwise, and for that reason, children must know that they are worthy of their own self-investment.

■ Action One: Talking Money

Eliminate language such as "crack down," "cutting back," and "tightening the belt." From the moment those words leave your lips, your child is no longer listening. Instead, together with your child, observe financial television and radio programs and discuss financial news of the day. On a weekly basis, assign your child the task of choosing a financial news headline to discuss, and talk about how that story impacts your family.

While you are spending a pleasant moment with your children, explain to them your change of heart. For example, you might say, "I've decided to make a change. I think sometimes we shop online too much and don't keep track of our expenditures. It is my responsibility as your parent to support you in becoming a millionaire. I never had the opportunity as a child to start saving, but if we start saving now, you can absolutely do it. Saving and investing money are activities that you and I can do as a team. And we're going to start today. Any questions?" In the rare instance that your child begins pouting, walk away. Continue to talk to your child about this only when he is calm.

■ Action Two: Establish a Family Business

Explore family business ideas and the associated responsibilities, financial investments, and legal ramifications.

Whether or not your family has been established as a legal entity, families tend to function financially as businesses, sometimes operating at a surplus and other times at a deficit (or at a profit or a loss). Children almost never view their own families as the business operations that they are.

- ❯ Have family members add their loose change to a money jar at the end of each day. Assign your child the task of counting the money regularly.
- ❯ Assign your child the task of totaling up your monthly bills.
- ❯ Together with your child, research websites such as www.lower mybills.com to find ideas for decreasing household expenses.
- ❯ Elicit feedback from your child about services that your family is paying for but not using.

■ Action Three: Establish a Golden Family Nest Egg

Have a family dinner together at least five times per week to strengthen unity and set savings goals. Use websites such as www.smartypig.com, which offers a complimentary online piggy bank for parents and young people to save for specific goals.

The best time to begin saving was twenty years ago; the second best time to begin is *now*. Teach your child the phenomenal power of growing her money (better known as "compounding"), and she can be a millionaire in her lifetime.

The last life reality that children think about is retirement. Perhaps because parents are closer to that period in life, they are—or should be—planning for how they will survive when they are no longer in the workforce. Despite the fact that their own retirements may be a long way off, children need to learn discipline and patience. No matter the age of your child, now is the time for him to begin long-term saving; to help him do so, set up a high-compound-interest savings account from which money is never taken out.

Teach children that saving is the key to building wealth. Modeling the behaviors of financially successful people will teach children that the rich are rich because they spend less than they earn and they save more of their income than other people tend to. Teach children to adopt a long-term view of how money accumulates.

Explain to your children that compound interest is money that one is paid, in addition to the original interest, by your banking institution. No one can afford to ignore free money. Many adults have asked, "Who cares about getting only 3.5 percent interest? I don't have time to care about pennies." Children should be taught that while growth in a high-yield account will not be impressive in the short term, over the course of thirty years she will truly see the results of her golden egg.

Children need to learn that getting rich can occur slowly through the miracle of compound interest. Parents and children alike often procrastinate on taking action, thinking, "I will start saving next year or after I receive my income tax refund." Procrastination and ignoring the power of compound interest can be costly. However, by using compound interest, parents can teach their children that with time they can absolutely be financially secure.

Using Bankrate.com, identify the bank or credit union in your area that pays the highest percentage rate of compound interest. Time is a valuable ally for children, which is all the more reason for children to learn these action points now. Suggested high-yield accounts are Roth IRAs, certificates of deposit (CDs), and the more conservative savings accounts.

To show the value of starting a savings plan early, the following chart outlines the growth fifteen-year-old Cassandra will see at age sixty-five if she puts her babysitting money in a Roth IRA averaging an 8 percent annual return. The chart indicates what will accumulate if Cassandra starts with a one-time contribution of $5,000 and makes no withdrawals or deposits after the initial deposit.

Age at which Cassandra deposits $5,000	Amount in her account at age sixty-five
Age fifteen	$14,000
Age thirty-five	$8,400
Age forty-five	$5,600

There is no avoiding reality. It is very costly to delay starting to save. Start *now*.

■ Action Four: Form a 10 Percent Club

> **Veronica's Story**
>
> Veronica is a thirty-five-year-old mother of one son.
>
> "For most of my life, I have dreaded the word 'budget.' In financial advice books, when I read about the importance of establishing a budget, my stomach would tighten in knots. I know where this comes from. I feel as if I am being denied the pleasures of life every time it is suggested that I budget. And I have passed this emotion to my son, who wants everything he sees. When I say 'budget,' he pouts.
>
> "But because I want a better life for him, I want Jason to invest in himself. And we can do it together by saving, as a start, 10 percent of my income and the same percentage of money gifts he receives from his grandmother and family members. I want the impulse to automatically save to be as natural to Jason as his and my impulses are to spend."

The first rule of money has always been to pay yourself first. Ask children which American president is on the face of any denomination of currency, and you might see their eyes glaze over as they gaze off into the distance. This facial expression primarily stems from the fact that they have never had a bill in their hands long enough to investigate. At a WorldofMoney.org orientation, when a group of young people were asked about the purpose of money, they answered in unison, "Spend it!" Young people have apparently formed a thriving Spending Club, but now it is time to form the 10 Percent Club. Membership requires that each child is shown how money grows and how money flows.

Many people think that paying oneself first means taking 10 percent of their income and splurging on a fancy dinner or a brand-new electronic device. However, with that mindset, people are not paying themselves first; they are paying the restaurant or retailer first. In order to qualify as paying oneself first, these monies must be deposited into a savings or money market account. You should determine a long-term goal for this money—for example, saving for a down payment to invest in real estate.

Parents may resist encouraging their children to do what they have found difficult or nearly impossible to do themselves. Children can probably remember when their parents have openly complained about money running short on one occasion or another. But parents can prevent their children from experiencing this by encouraging them to save 10 percent of whatever money they earn. They can spell out the long-term effects of their children's mindlessly wasting money on trinkets—financial bondage—and instead cement in their children the mindset of long-term savers.

The freedom that comes from knowing they are teaching their children to provide for themselves, regardless of life's obstacles, is the dream for every mindful parent. When your child forms a 10 Percent Club, she learns that being financially independent and secure is more important than impressing her classmates, who may struggle with their own personal finance issues. And the earlier a child develops this saving muscle, the stronger her ability to create her own nest egg will be. (Equally important is that children should be taught to set aside time for family before their jobs or friends. Family, spiritual, and physical health must always come before achieving material possessions.)

Parents should follow the below guidelines with their 10 Percent Club:

- The 10 Percent Club should include all family members.
- Set a financial goal. For example, your thirteen-year-old may determine to save a certain amount per month or per year in order to make a certain purchase or build up a nest egg. Parents should ask their children to calculate how much of their 10 percent they will need to set aside in order achieve that particular financial goal.
- Children should devise an earning strategy plan that lays out how they will earn money. Of course, many children would prefer that their money come from their parents and extended family members, without them having to work for it. While parents

are saving for their child's college educations, they should require that children brainstorm about their own incomes.

❍ Ten percent of all money that comes to your child from outside the nuclear family unit (gifts from grandparents, uncles, aunts, and favorite cousins, for example) must be tagged for this club.

❍ Determine that the 10 Percent monies must not be touched until a long-term date in the future.

Discussion Points

❍ Ask your child how he feels about the amount of money he might have saved if, a year ago, he had begun putting away two dollars every day.

❍ Explore what he would have done with his imaginary savings.

■ Action Five: Teach Children to Fish

"Give a man a fish and you have fed him for a day. Teach a man to fish and you have fed him for a lifetime." —LAO-TZU

Griffin's Story

Griffin, a thirty-three-year-old construction manager, has three teen-age daughters.

"My daughters must have been queens of their own kingdoms in a past life, because I don't know where they get their entitlement attitudes. Their friends are from middle- to upper-middle-class families who are in as much debt as we are, but whatever my wife and I provide, my daughters want more. Work? My daughters have never gotten their hands dirty."

Douglas's Story

Douglas, the father of Nicholas, thirteen, and Anna, twelve, was laid off from his job as a sales and marketing manager three years ago. The two siblings are more than willing to contribute to the household by taking odd jobs; however, Douglas refuses to allow them to work. He believes it is his duty to provide for his family. "I'll never let a child of mine support me. How would that make me look as a father and a husband?"

Parents like Griffin need to enforce layered standards with their daughters, based upon the principle that money is to be earned. In addition to learning that performing well in school is their occupation, many entitled children need to experience how their financial support is earned.

Lauren, a corporate attorney, shares, "From my earliest memory, my parents eagerly taught us the family business. This is where I learned my work ethic, watching my parents work, often twelve- to sixteen-hour days, but still having affection and playtime for me and my brothers. After homework and on weekends, even though I had to stand on a stool, I worked behind the counter at the family's hardware store. My father taught me how to process credit cards, count money in the cash register, and how to help customers. This early exposure into my family's business made me feel that I was contributing something. Though the hardware store was profitable, there were slow times, and I knew what kind of Christmas our family was going to have in terms of gifts. But no matter if we had a slow period for the business, my parents would find enough to donate turkeys to the local food bank. And every holiday until I left for college, I would serve families who were less fortunate. So with my own children, I plan to teach them the same thing so that they won't feel they are entitled to anything without rolling up their sleeves and earning it."

It is important, especially with young children, to show where you earn your income. Without this experience, children see you depart each day for a magical place called work, not knowing that this location is where you perform the responsibilities that enable you to financially provide for your family.

Many companies have a Take Your Child to Work Day during which tours and workshops are conducted. If your workplace has this, consider designing an activity centered on the financial aspects of your company's operation. Have children meet the chief executive officer, the chief financial officer, and the accountants and visit the payroll department. Children should be introduced to the world of money through professionals who work in the arena.

If your company does not have a Take Your Child to Work Day, consult with your human resources department to see if one can be organized. Parents can also organize tours of local businesses, where owners can explain how their businesses and their families operate.

Time to Fish

Guiding children to becoming entrepreneurs will instill responsibility, creativity, and professionalism. Children who are taught how money is earned, saved, and invested can then participate in on-the-job training by creating their own businesses. Eleven-year-old Em-Peress began earning her own money by launching a dog-walking business in her neighborhood. Her mother, Adrienne, shares, "At first, Em-Peress would spend every nickel her business earned, but when we created a spreadsheet detailing how much money she has thrown away, her attitude dramatically transformed."

Siblings William, Daniel, Serina, and Ciana launched Three's a Party, a New Jersey–based DJ and party-planning business, after receiving encouragement from their parents. The brothers and sisters noticed that there was an absence of safe activities for teens in their town. They met with their parents and requested a $600 investment so that they could purchase equipment for a new business. Three's a Party became an instant success, and within six months of operation, the siblings received a business contract with their city. Their father, John, remarks, "Working in the criminal justice system, I see on a daily basis what happens when parents do not invest in their children. So when my kids want to make a business investment, there is no way my wife and I can deny them. Our children are building their future, and we will support them."

In another example, Leanna Archer founded her company, Hair Inc., when she was eight years old, and later made *Inc.* magazine's 30 Under 30 list, which features successful young entrepreneurs. Using a family formula for hair repair, she began her career by selling her product to fellow students. The buzz spread quickly, and soon orders were coming from stores and customers across the country. Meanwhile, Leanna still found the time to develop new products and make the honor roll in middle school. At age twelve, she was offered a scholarship to attend Harvard. Still, Leanna saves half of her earnings in order to afford Harvard Law School. She also delivers motivational speeches for parents about communication skills and for teens about living their dreams and starting their own business. Leanna also founded the Leanna Archer Education Foundation, a nonprofit organization dedicated to helping children in Haiti.

Then there is the undercover chief executive officer Jasmine Lawrence, who founded Eden Body Works when she was eleven years old. Jasmine saved the millions of dollars her business generated to study robotics at Georgia Tech. Now a college junior, she hired a management team for her business while she makes an impact on the world through computers and technology.

No matter what their children's business idea, from operating their own lemonade stand to starting an Internet-based business, parents would be wise to teach them to fish rather than simply giving them fish. This will instill seeds of happiness, success, and prosperity in their lives. Giving your children the opportunity to learn how to operate their own business, together with your faith in them, will enable children to learn from their victories and mistakes.

Children and Allowance

> *"The easiest way to teach children the value of money is to borrow some from them."* —GEORGE BERNARD SHAW

Parents often have contrasting views on whether or not their children should receive allowances. Viewpoints range from "My child should not be paid to do her chores" to "I use paying for household chores and giving my child a modest allowance as a basis for an early education about money." The purpose of an allowance is not to persuade children to contribute to their family's financial well-being. The purpose of an allowance is to teach children about money management and should be kept separate from completing household chores.

Children should be given an allowance beginning around age seven, but it should not be connected with helping around the household or academic performance. Parents should guide their children not solely with regard to spending their allowances but also with respect to establishing savings goals. This will give parents the opportunity to introduce the concept of paying oneself first. Should the child fail to complete a household chore, the parent should suspend a privilege, such as the viewing of a favorite television program. The amount of the allowance should vary according to the family's finances.

There are four caveats that should be explored:

1. Parents should discuss with their children their responsibility for managing and safeguarding their own allowances. It is important for parents to be aware of their children's expenditures and to make sure that their purchases reflect the family's values. Parents should also teach children to save 10 percent of all the money they receive.
2. Children should not be expected to cover costs for necessities such as rent, food, and education.
3. As in life, children should learn to account for how their allowance is spent.

4. A child's allowance should be allocated on a scheduled basis. Should the child choose to spend their allowance and request an advance on the next installment, the parent is advised to refuse.

Spreading Wings

Though many children dream of leaving home and beginning life on their own, they rarely consider how they will pay for it. Then there are other young people who never plan to become financially responsible, especially when they have enabling parents. These children believe their parents' money will always be there for them—that is, until parents announce that it won't.

Raymond's sixteen-year-old daughter, Monica, called her mother crying after he discussed his plans for her. "Daddy wants to get rid of me. He wants to kick me out of the house." Hiding her chuckle on the other end of the telephone, Monica's mother explained, "Your father and I love you and are not kicking you out of the house. We just want to make sure that you are equipped with the resources you need for when you do go out on your own."

Lawrence and Donald's Story

Lawrence and Donald are twin twenty-six-year-olds who still live in the bedroom they were raised in as children. While their absentee father was a career criminal, their dear mother, Rita, worked three full-time jobs to support her sons (even into adulthood) and their father; the three men only work odd jobs when they choose to. They believe that Rita and all women exist solely to provide for their financial needs. Lawrence and Donald frequently argue with their mother when she attempts to challenge their erroneous belief that they are the heads of the household; but still, their mother refuses to force them to leave. Though she is the sole income earner, she believes that her unemployed, uneducated adult sons will one day magically mature.

Many parents have separation pangs when they think of the day when their child will leave the nest. But alas, that day will and must come. Parents can empower their children by discussing this eventuality at age-appropriate intervals.

Eagle Legacy

An Eagle Legacy should be started when children are between the ages of nine and twelve. In nature, the eagle parent stirs up the nest so that her eaglets do not grow comfortable. Similarly, parents can implement their Eagle Legacy with questions such as these: When you grow up, what will your house look like? What kind of career will you need to be successful at in order to pay the mortgage for that house? What do you need to study in school in order to have that career? What do you think we'll find if we go house hunting on the Internet?

Now be forewarned that your child, whether she is eight or eighteen, may glance at you as if you have taken leave of your senses. But you should remain confident that the eagle is one member of the bird family that provides a great example of financial parenting.

By contrast, nature also offers poor examples for financial parenting, in which the youngsters remain dependent on their parents.

Ostrich Parents

The child of an Ostrich Parent is protected from his negative actions and is often left in precarious situations, only to be rescued and then go on to repeat his actions. The Ostrich Parent allows her child to dictate his desires and is open for discussion about what her child wants to do with the parent's finances.

Nina, a frustrated, forty-five-year-old divorced mother, allows her daughter to tell her what to purchase for her. "I must stop allowing my daughter to tell me what she will and will not wear. Of course, I want her to feel she can come to me to ask for things—yet her tone of voice suggests that I work for her. Since I am her sole financial support, I think my daughter's approach could be more respectful and have more gratitude. Instead, it is the other way around. Because her father is not in her life, my guilt is trying to replace his absence. But what I have created is a monster."

If you are the type of parent who wants his twenty-five-, thirty-five-, or forty-year-old child still sleeping in the same bedroom in which they were first burped, then you have adopted the Ostrich Plan. Face it—your little cutie-pie does not want to leave your nest. Who would? Under your roof, your little darling depends on your generosity for her financial well-being. Not to mention that you also throw in free rent, delicious home-cooked meals, and clean laundry. Heck, you all are family, so you might as well do it, you rationalize—that is, if you consider the consequences at all. Perhaps, you argue, this state of affairs is only the result of these hard economic times. Though he or she is now thirty years old, you like living with your adult child, and you will not push her to become financially self-reliant until she is ready.

May I be candid? You have your head in the sand. You are not quite sure when or how will be the good time for your child to become financially responsible. Here's the answer: *now*.

Chicken-Hearted Parents

Chicken-hearted, well-meaning parents behave timidly toward their children. The Chicken-Hearted Parenting approach allows a child to ravage a parent's finances, often coaxing the parent to overdraw his savings account. These children may have had their own funds that they used to support the lifestyle they believe they are entitled to. This child may have been caught stealing money from family members. Not every family member trusts this child around his or her wallet. Though the child's behavior is common knowledge, the Chicken-Hearted Parent allows the child to continue on her rampage.

Alberta, a fifty-two-year-old grandmother, has been supporting her adult son and her granddaughter. They live next door in a two-family townhouse, but their tentacles reach through the walls and into Alberta's wallet.

"When I gave my son the down payment to purchase this house, I breathed a sigh of relief. I thought, Finally I can get my life back. Well, that lasted about two years. He was paying his share of the mortgage, and I was paying mine. Then come to find out that he did not place a down payment and used half the money to invest in some get-rich-quick scheme with his friend who just got out of prison. He used the other half to buy brand-new furniture and a flat-screen television set in every room. I thought his business must be doing very well, but it was my money my son was using. Next thing I know I am getting foreclosure notices, the bank is calling me, and my son is crying on my doorstep. Though I love my son and granddaughter, I don't want them living with me, so I had to go into my retirement to bail him out. Now that I think about it, he did the same thing with the money his daddy left him. Ran through $50,000 in six months. I don't want to make excuses for him, but I think he is doing the best he can."

Chicken Parents often grapple with children who push against the boundaries of the parent-child relationship. Enabled by a doting parent and unable to accept responsibility for their own lives, these children can destroy their parent's financial well-being. Chicken Parents should cut the apron strings and adopt the strategy of the Eagle by teaching their children sound financial principles, pointing them in the direction of earning their own income, and then allowing them to fly on their own. Yes, adult children may stumble, and they may fall. But left to the law of self-preservation, adult children absolutely will rise up and fly on their own and will gain newfound self-respect.

Janet, age twenty-nine and a mother of three, says, "When my mother told me I had ninety days to move out of her house, I thought she was joking. I moved back to my mother's house for the third time, had been there for over one year, and was reverting back to my childish, selfish behavior. In reflection, I now understand that my mother taught me to stand up in my life, raise my own children, but I took her for granted by expecting her to babysit my children and paying toward the mortgage when I felt like it. She had every right to require that I be responsible for the life I created. And particularly with her health issues, my mother deserves better from me. I want her to see that I can fly on my own."

Proverbs 24:16 declares, "A righteous man falls seven times—but he rises up again." Parents must learn how to tell—and show—their children, "You may be knocked down, but that doesn't mean you have to be knocked out."

Eagle Parents

When loving parents become loving eagles, embracing the importance and imperative of their role in their children's financial education, only then will our families, communities, and world truly change. The Eagle Parent knows that if her child is not taught how to be financially responsible as a child, he will be unable to be financially responsible when he is out in the world on his own.

Eagle Parents topple their nests, particularly if their child resists being taught, yet parents should remain near enough to make sure their children do not fall off the edge of the financial cliff. If they do, the Eagle Parent must not rescue the child with more gifts of money but should protect the child if he or she encounters physical harm. The Eagle Parent swoops down and stands her child back on his own feet—*outside* of the nest—all the while offering words of encouragement and faith that he or she can be a great saver, a smart investor, and a person of service to the world.

By her supportive presence, an Eagle Parent reminds her child that all is not lost when she does not receive a new pair of sneakers, is required to contribute financially to the household, or is expected to map out a plan to a secure retirement. Your children will reflect your seriousness in these endeavors. Once you spread your determined wings, your children will recognize that the financial honeymoon is over, and they will know they can model your Eagle behavior.

■ Action Six: Raising Philanthropists

In today's world, when charitable engagement is needed more than ever, a child should never have the opportunity to say, "I'm bored." Instead, parents should require that their children engage in some form of philanthropy from an early age. After visiting East Africa, two Stanford University students, Matt Flannery and Jessica Jackley, decided to create an online resource to help alleviate poverty. The two created an opportunity for those who live in the developed world to loan to those in Africa who want to start their own businesses. Thus Kiva was launched in 2005. With a repayment rate of 98 percent, as of March 31, 2012, Kiva has distributed $300,209,450 in loans from 744,558 lenders.

Oprah Winfrey chose not to rest on her laurels as a television mogul. Instead, disturbed by the epidemic of apathy that permeated US school systems, Winfrey launched the Oprah Winfrey Leadership Academy for Girls in South Africa. In a 2007 *Newsweek* magazine interview, she commented, "Say what you will about the American educational system—it does work. . . . If you are a child in the United States, you can get an education. I became so frustrated with visiting inner-city schools that I just stopped going. The sense that you need to learn just isn't there. If you ask the kids what they want or need, they will say an iPod, sneakers, or some money. In South Africa, they don't ask for money or toys. They ask for uniforms so they can go to school."

Parents from so-called nonaffluent families often believe that families must be wealthy in order to become philanthropists. The good news is that is not the case. Perhaps influenced by the announcement that billionaires Bill Gates and Warren Buffett will donate the majority of their wealth to charity, high-asset families are now seeking guidance on how to raise their children to serve the world. One added advantage of your child's being financially responsible is he or she can turn this powerful currency into a force for doing good. Children want to be given the opportunity to contribute to the world, and doing so will bolster their self-esteem.

Throughout history, the generosity of modest wage earners as well as the wealthy has been responsible for supporting historic African American human and civil rights organizations. The following queries can serve as guideposts for you to help develop a service-minded child. Ask your child:

- How do you wish to serve the world?
- What problems do you wish did not exist?
- How do you feel when you see children who are less fortunate?
- Whose responsibility is it to make the world a better place?
- Do you know any children your age who volunteer in their neighborhoods?
- What can we as a family do on a regular basis to serve?
- How do you think you will feel if you help others?
- How do you think others will feel if you help them?
- What is the difference between charity and service?
- How do you think community service will improve your selection of colleges and careers?

Parents should require that their children volunteer in their local community or create foundations to address issues they would like to support. Take Erica Bee, an African American teenager from Arizona who founded Darfur Tucson, an organization dedicated to educating her peers about ending the genocide in the Sudan. In the *Arizona Jewish Post*, Erica said, "I will continue my fight for an end to the Darfur genocide by educating students, teaching individual responsibility, and encouraging them to stand up for what they believe is right." Erica's volunteerism does not end with Darfur. She also volunteers escorting Holocaust survivors around the Tucson Jewish Community Center and created a program called Students Making a Difference.

Then there is shy, eleven-year-old Sienna Gonzalez, who lost her otherwise healthy young father after he succumbed to metastatic lung cancer. Tragically, Sienna's mother was later diagnosed with pancreatic cancer. Sienna and her mother learned that the Pancreatic Cancer Action Network was planning an advocacy day in Washington, DC, to seek legislative support for the Pancreatic Cancer Research and Education Act. Without telling her mother, Sienna asked her classmates, and then her school, and then her entire community to sign the petition. Through her fears and bewilderment, Sienna has developed compassion beyond her years. "I want to save my mom, but if I can't save my mom, maybe I'll save somebody," she said.

Some WorldofMoney.org youth and their supportive parents collected over one thousand pairs of shoes to be donated to poor children in rural Liberia. Eight-year-old Stefan remarked, "I want to help other children who don't have as much as I do, so I will continue to collect shoes to send to the schools in Liberia. That is what is being part of the world of money is all about."

Nine-year-old Joshua Smith was concerned about his cash-strapped city of Detroit and decided to launch a lemonade and popcorn stand to contribute. He made $3,600 and was given the Spirit of Detroit Award for his philanthropy. Detroit mayor David Bing earmarked the donation to improve a playground near Joshua's home.

Children who are engaged in changing their world lack the time to be swayed by consumerism. By channeling their children's desire away from consumerism and toward improving their communities, parents establish the foundation from which to raise a philanthropist. Through their dedicated efforts, young philanthropists focus their resources on eradicating problems in the world as well as bonding with their families.

Gandhi once said, "Be the change you wish to see in the world." Young people need to be raised as change makers rather than wait for someone else to rescue them. Now, more than ever, parents and young people alike should stop relying on outside sources to rescue them or solve their dilemmas. Within each child lies the capacity to bring forth innovative concepts to create thriving, sustaining communities.

Parents should spontaneously discuss with their children their own financial donations to public charities, highlighting the purpose of these donations and how emboldened they feel about financially supporting a worthy cause. Parents should require that their children research a variety of different causes and organizations and decide as a family which they will support. Children should invite their friends to participate in their philanthropic activities to help others to empower themselves.

Tour your local community and identify the nonprofit organizations that serve your neighbors. Children should learn not to take their presence for granted out of ignorance or because of a lack of support. Keep in mind that everyone can donate some amount of money, no matter how meager their earnings. Nothing can enter a closed fist.

■ Action Seven: Delayed Gratification Strategy

Shannon, a married father and a deacon at his church, feels encouraged when reading the biblical scripture, John 10:10: "Beloved, I pray that you may prosper in all things and be in health, just as your soul prospers. Jesus came so we can have life to the full."

Shannon believes that his well-meaning mother raised him to be a financial martyr and to reject living a prosperous life. "My mother believed that the Lord would take care of our finances, that money was akin to the devil, whatever that meant. But when I became a member of a new church family that preaches that living a financially responsible and prosperous life is what our God wanted for us, I was moved to tears that I could pass this teaching on to my children."

All religions and spiritual disciplines address the promise of prosperity in one's life—that is, planned prosperity. In the practice of Buddhism, Gautama Buddha cautions, "One is the path that leads to material wealth; the other is the path that leads to nirvana."[1]

Seizing control of your finances is the proper application of all spiritual practices. All disciplines have an underlying theme that is reflected in the popular hymn "God Bless the Child." As a parent, you need not cease purchasing gifts that you can afford, but you should understand the emotional impulses that drive your willingness to indulge your children. Author James W. Frick once wrote, "Don't tell me where your priorities are. Show me where you spend your money and I'll tell you what they are." Teaching your children to take control begins with showing them that responsibility begins with being aware of one's goals and current debt. Children who are

---

1. Gautama Buddha (Dhammapada 5:75).

taught that money only exists to be spent are being guided down the wrong life path.

If children meet their responsibilities, if they are respectful, and if there is extra money in your budget, then by all means, purchase whatever you know will warm their hearts, as long as the purchase adheres to your value system. Keep in mind, though, that parents do not need to materially reward their children for every positive behavior. But rewards should be based on the child's performance, and they should teach children the balance of living as a consumer and as an investor. For example, if your child asks to purchase a new pair of jeans (specifically, the brand all of his friends are wearing), then you should ask if your child has researched the stock price of the company that produces the item.

You should not feel guilty about not buying a product if you:

❯ Do not approve of the product or service
❯ Would be purchasing the product out of misguided obligation or to prevent your child's temper tantrum
❯ Would need to purchase expensive accessories and software to achieve basic functionality, making the initial purchase cost-prohibitive
❯ Would put yourself in a precarious financial position by doing so

When you reject your child's request for a particular purchase, you should calmly explain, "I much prefer to use the money for a better investment." You can also challenge your children to earn money to make their own purchases. But in all cases, children must be taught that the family business must save 3 to 10 percent of its gross income. Even if the amount is small, it can be saved.

There is much power in repetition. As you repeat the steps outlined in your action plans, you will reprogram your money style. Seizing control and releasing beliefs based in a sense of scarcity will draw you toward innovative ways to change your child's financial legacy.

▪ Right-on-the-Money Review

- ❯ Action One: Talking Money
- ❯ Action Two: Establish a Family Business
- ❯ Action Three: Establish a Golden Family Nest Egg
- ❯ Action Four: Form a 10 Percent Club
- ❯ Action Five: Teach Children to Fish
- ❯ Action Six: Raising Philanthropists
- ❯ Action Seven: Delayed Gratification Strategy

10

The Family as a Business

■ Get Started

Today is the day you and your children sit down and start a new business: the business of your family household. To start you off on the right track, we'll use the five tenets of the WorldofMoney.org Youth Financial Education Institute:

1. Learn
2. Earn
3. Save
4. Invest
5. Donate

■ Learn

In a perfect world, all parents would impart sound financial principles to their children. But we do not live in a perfect world. Many parents, through no fault of their own, were never taught how to manage money themselves. But today, because of their love for their children and their determination that their children have a better life than they did, parents need to encourage their children to become financially responsible with their support.

Remember your last vacation to a foreign destination? You may have studied the language of the country so that you could interact with new friends and immerse yourself in the culture. Friends or blogs may have shared tips on the best method to navigate your destination. Well, these same methods should be adopted with your immersion voyage to the world of money. This strange new world has a mindset, behaviors, and a language all its own. Similar to the subtle differences an American English speaker will notice when visiting England or a Dominican Spanish speaker will notice in Spain, the language of the world of money is full of nuance, homonyms, and uncommon terms. (For example, the term "investment vehicle" does not refer to an automobile.) You and your children should make an effort to learn this new language.

- ❯ Together with your children, read and watch financial media outlets on a daily basis. When a new word is introduced, research the definition. You and your children will find that the more you tune into the language used in the world of money, the more you will understand.
- ❯ Together with your children, schedule a visit with your bank representative. Request a presentation on the various financial products that your branch provides. Schedule a conference call with any representative who has access to your finances. Many adults tend to ignore the health of their money, but we must all take an active interest in the details, including the financial institutions where our money is housed.
- ❯ Enroll in a financial or business seminar at least twice annually. When appropriate, bring your children. Discuss your experience with your children.

■ Earn

Most of today's successful business owners began their careers as teenagers. Ajani Nyabingi has been the owner of Ajani's Bicycle

Repair shop in his Queens neighborhood since he was thirteen years old. Being mechanically inclined, Ajani combined his passion for solving problems with his talent for repairing bikes, and this straight-A student became an entrepreneur. Fourteen-year-old Nashana Yates launched Hair By Nashana in the basement of her family's home. Nashana has developed her own clientele from her classmates and friends.

If your child is like most young people, he would like to earn his own money, but job opportunities may be limited in your area. Not to worry, though—if you can dream it, you can achieve it (a money-making opportunity, that is). Passion, discipline, and talent combine to create a successful entrepreneur.

Have your child survey your neighborhood. What service do adults need that is not already being provided? Examples might include walking dogs, mowing lawns, shoveling snow, tutoring, babysitting, running errands, washing cars, blogging, or developing websites for small businesses. Your child might set up a lemonade stand near sports events or sell candy at school. As with any venture, discussing plans as a family is important so that parents can guide young people through setting up their business. (You might begin by visiting the business-consulting websites listed in the "Recommended Resources" section on page 201 of this book.)

■ Save

How Rich Youth Think

Affluent youth have often benefited from legacies of financial education that their families have built up over generations. Whether they've used their money wisely or not, wealthy young people have been introduced to the financial concepts by which their families continue to grow their fortunes. In general, these young people possess diversified investment portfolios consisting of mutual funds, bonds, stocks, and real estate. And, more important, their family members are successful entrepreneurs and active philanthropists. These visionary teen millionaires possess unique mindsets and behaviors, as outlined in the following points:

- Teen millionaires do not wear the names of other people on their backs. They produce products that others use.
- Teen millionaires learn how to manage their money by saving, investing, and donating.
- Teen millionaires see their academic educations as investments in themselves.
- Teen millionaires contribute time and money to causes that improve the world.
- Teen millionaires did not all come from wealthy families.
- Teen millionaires create their own businesses, some of which serve global markets.
- The next teen millionaire is starting now, saving now, and getting to work now!
- Black teen millionaires do not blame the white man, the government, or their parents for their own financial behavior. They take complete responsibility for their spending and saving.

While rappers are "making it rain" on their way to bankruptcy court, the next teen mogul is researching and creating the next product or service that might change the world. Their behavior stems from their prosperous or "have" way of thinking rather than from a "have not" mindset.

First of all, those with a mogul mindset are not told by outside forces when and how to spend their money. Now more than ever, young people need to hit the reset button on their relationships with money. Though many young people admit that the economic recession has affected the amount of money they have access to, this age group continues to use a high degree of disposable dollars and engage in very little saving. According to Buzz Marketing, 86 percent of teens believe they have learned valuable lessons from the crisis, yet 53 percent intend to resume their reckless spending once they believe the financial crisis is over.

Newsflash: squandering money is not a behavior to resort back to. Those with prosperous mindsets would never participate in making such poor financial decisions.

▪ Invest

Hazel's Story

Hazel is forty-two years old and the mother of three children. She says, "My mother used most of her money to help extended family members but never used the money to help our family. Some positive financial behaviors I have shown to my children include investing money in empowering them and making sure they are supported in their endeavors. The bad part is that I have not saved enough money for emergencies and vacations. If I had to rewrite my personal financial history from the last fifteen to twenty years, I would have invested sooner in an IRA and a mutual fund. When I received my severance package from my last job, I received an extensive amount of money, which included my 401(k) and pension. It allowed me to work part-time and raise my daughters. I don't regret that part, but I really should have used it to make more money. Instead of depleting my funds, I would have been letting the money work for me.

"Now that I know my mother was more of a financial martyr for everyone else, I am getting better at discussing personal finance with my children. I am happy they are open to the discussion."

Invest in a high-interest investment product today, such as a Roth IRA or a certificate of deposit. Consult with your children and review the "Recommend Resources" section (page 201) for ideas on where to get started. Take action in small increments every day. Make investing as natural as brushing your teeth.

Poverty Mindsets Ripped from the Headlines

"X-Box Shopper Pepper Sprays Twenty Customers on Black Friday"

"Shoppers Stampede and Kill a Store Security Guard"

"Police Use a Stun Gun on Violent Shopper"

"Thousands of Adult Shoppers Wait Outside Door for Midnight Shopping"

"Shoppers Fight Over $1.88 Towels"

"Grandfather Arrested for Shoplifting a Video Game"

■ Donate

This concept is all the more urgent as colleges, universities, and employers report that they prefer to admit and hire youth who have a consistent track record of community service. An admissions officer from a prestigious New York university shared, "Frankly, we want to develop future world leaders. And future world leaders are inspired to effect positive change in their locales, centered around issues they are most passionate about." Further, an examination of the lives of successful individuals reveals a pattern of community service through the donation of time or money.

Donate your time to charitable organizations and contribute possessions you no longer use. Visit www.dosomething.org, a website that can help you brainstorm and support causes in your community. Organizations such as the Girls Scouts and Boy Scouts are also known for supporting youth in value-creating projects.

Service Projects to Consider
- Park beautification
- Delivering meals to the ill or elderly
- Reading to senior citizens or children
- Volunteering at an animal shelter

- Spearheading a shoe or toy drive for children
- Organizing classmates and friends to donate money to organizations that support your city

■ Your Family, Inc.

Establishing a business is an excellent financial and entrepreneurial training tool for the entire family. Launching a family business can strengthen family ties and allow children to handle responsibilities. No matter the economic climate—whether a recession, a depression, or a stable, growing economy—smart parents should encourage their children to identify products or services their family can provide that satisfy the needs of others and earn them extra dollars.

In addition, family businesses instill in children the notion that they need not always seek employment but can become business owners. Because of the emotional relationships that exist, parents and children need to be clear about everyone's responsibilities in the family business, as well as the seriousness of this initiative.

Parents should follow these guidelines:

- Decide if the family business will be child-led or parent-led
- Never force a child to participate in the family business
- Recognize each child's personality strengths and weaknesses
- Establish defined roles for each person in the business (children's roles should be age-appropriate)
- Start a business the children are excited about
- Create a distinct family-business workspace
- Schedule nonbusiness time to unwind and enjoy one another's company

Ideas for family- or children-led businesses:

- Lawn service
- Senior care
- Pet sitting/walking
- Cleaning service

❯ Daycare
❯ Errand service
❯ Car wash
❯ Bicycle repair
❯ Catering and/or selling bake goods

■ Next Steps:

1. The child should identify the appropriate business type.
2. Name the business and visit a web-hosting site (like www .godaddy.com) to determine if the domain name is available.
3. Research the business and identify best practices and pitfalls.
4. With your children, create a mission statement, draw up a list of your family values, and identify target customers.
5. Put in writing the duties that each family member is responsible for (and be specific).
6. Determine, and put in writing, whether your business will operate on a seasonal, weekend, or after-school basis.
7. Each parent should commit and put in writing how much money he or she is willing to invest as well as the terms, if any, for repayment.
8. Parents should help children address compensation and identify a clear plan for dissolution of the business (all of which should be put in writing).
9. Write out an organizational chart and a plan for addressing conflicts, which identifies the family member who has the final say.
10. When you want to incorporate your business, contact your secretary of state and request the necessary forms. At a minimum, you will need to file a certificate of incorporation with the secretary of state. There may also be other forms to complete, but this will vary by state. Consult a lawyer if you have questions.
11. Consult with the Internal Revenue Service to determine the appropriate tax forms, filings, and possible deductions.

Parents can teach children to become independent by not mixing business issues with home life. All businesses begin with meager resources; thus parents should refrain from referring to their children's businesses as "their little business" or "something they're doing." The business, no matter the size, should be taken seriously and talked about accordingly.

Boundaries should also be established around if, how, and when your child may communicate with adults regarding the business, both in person and online. For safety's sake, parents may choose to represent their children when communicating with adult customers about the business.

■ Parent Prosperity Pledge

When I was young I thought that money was the most important thing in life; now that I am old I know that it is. —OSCAR WILDE

I will:

- Establish a family savings goal with my child
- Know myself, both my financial strengths and weaknesses
- Ignore the Joneses
- Engage in candid family discussions about finances and set goals
- Avoid financial competition with my child's other parent
- Teach my child the difference between their wants and their needs
- Remember that my child needs me, not things
- Watch, read, and discuss financial media coverage with my child
- Be a philanthropist and raise a philanthropist
- Allow my child to experience delayed gratification
- Accept that "no" and "I can't afford it" are appropriate and informative answers
- Teach my child the distinction between a "have" consciousness and "have not" consciousness

- Surround my family with financial experts
- Increase my financial vocabulary
- Learn, earn, save, invest, and donate
- Be a financial role model and avoid media-promoted, emotion-filled consumerism (for example, on Black Friday, I will remember the reason for the season)
- Remember that our government may or may not make fiscal changes, but I always have the choice and opportunity to do so

■ Youth Prosperity Pledge

I will:

- Establish a family savings goal with my parents
- Know myself, both my financial strengths and weaknesses
- Release my fear, shame, and ego
- Participate in candid family discussions about finances
- Avoid pitting my parents against each other or manipulating them
- Learn the difference between my wants and needs
- Accept that materialism does not validate me
- Watch, read, and discuss financial media coverage with my parents and friends
- Be a philanthropist and volunteer in my community
- Open and maintain a savings account
- Study the distinction between a "have" consciousness and a "have not" consciousness
- Know that celebrities are usually not good financial role models
- Expand my financial vocabulary
- Express appreciation
- Learn, earn, save, invest, and donate
- Be a financial role model and avoid media-promoted, emotion-filled consumerism
- Remember that our government may or may not make fiscal changes, but I always have the choice and opportunity to do so

11

Invaded Nesters

"You cannot build character and courage by taking away man's initiative and independence." —ABRAHAM LINCOLN

Harris and Joy's Story

Harris is sixty-two, and Joy is fifty-nine.

"Not only did our grown child move back in our house after she was laid off, she brought two babies with her," Harris explains. "Now we love her and all, but we are approaching our golden years. Our in-house babysitting days were long behind us, or so we thought. My wife and I adore our grandchildren—but from a distance and when we want to. Before they moved back in, we liked to love them up and spoil them and then send them back to their mother over in West Orange, New Jersey. Now we have to send them down the hall to the same bedroom their mother was reared in.

"Even though my daughter has a new job, she has not offered one dime to support the household. It is going on nine months, and I am ready to pack their things and put them out. This was supposed to be our special time where we take our dream vacations or cruise around the world. But my wife wants to continue treating our daughter like she is in high school, and I don't know what to do. My neighbor's son lives at home, except he never left and he is forty years old. Short of selling our house, I don't know how to get rid of my own daughter."

■ When Children Come Home to Roost

Due to difficult economic conditions, millions of parents have allowed their adult children to return to their childhood homes. But allowing adult children to live with their parents for extended periods of time contradicts the role of an Eagle Parent.

Remember the Empty Nest Syndrome you felt when you heard the loud silence in your home after your youngest adult child moved out on his own? In the early days, you professed loneliness, saying that you missed the sound of the children who had once filled your home. For a time, it was just you, or perhaps you and your spouse. But after a few years, your child moved back in, and now you have conflicting emotions.

Do not be alarmed, dear parent: you are not alone. According to a poll for the National Endowment for Financial Education conducted by Harris Interactive, 40 percent of American adults ages eighteen to thirty-nine either live at home or have done so in the recent past. According to a joint study by Princeton and the Brookings Institute,[1] in 2007 black and Latino young adults, as well as those in every age bracket, were more likely to live with their parents than the general population. Further, black adult men live with their parents more than black adult women in every age bracket, including whites. The number of black adults in residence with parents continues to make dramatic

---

1. Princeton-Brookings Institute, *The Future of Children: Transition to Adulthood* 20, no. 1, Spring 2010.

leaps, particularly for young adults in their twenties and young adults of foreign-born parents.

The numbers show that black parents are more likely to have adult children living under their roof (because they have returned or because they never left), so it is imperative to set house rules as a condition of their tenancy. Parents have a right to expect that their adult children contribute financially to the household and the overall maintenance of the home. That being said, parents should plan an exit strategy with their children, and the adult child and parent must agree to respect each other as adults. Because the home belongs to the parent, who has ultimate authority, the relationship is mutually beneficial only if the adult child behaves as an adult and not an adult regressed back into a child's mindset.

Unless parents want to play Rosie the Maid for the rest of their lives, they must resist the temptation to coddle their children. While providing emotional support and faith in their abilities is important, parents need to resist being automatic teller machines for adult children. If your adult children already have negative money habits, bestowing no-strings-attached money on them will only cripple them further. And do not even think about subsidizing their social lives or their whims out of love.

In *The Millionaire Next Door*, authors Thomas Stanley and William Danko write, "Adults who sit around waiting for the next dose of economic outpatient care are typically not very productive. The more wealth parents accumulate, the more economically disciplined their adult children are likely to be." There is a marked distinction between adults who live with their parents, without financially contributing, and those who succeed through life's victories and defeats. A truly loving parent will encourage the latter outcome rather than the former.

Understanding that anyone can find himself or herself in an economic crisis, parents can contribute some amount to help a struggling adult child. However, parents must be clear that their home cannot be used like a hotel during an all-expenses-paid vacation.

To offset entitlement issues and power struggles, parents and adult children should clarify their expectations, keeping the following points in mind:

❯ Because financial issues are what landed the adult child under his parent's roof, the parent should require that the child enroll in a financial education course, lest he be doomed to repeat his financial mistakes. Organizations that provide individual financial counseling, such as the Financial Clinic (www.thefinancial clinic.org), are a good choice.

❯ Parents should remember that before returning home, their adult child has matured and possibly reshaped her personality. Therefore, the parent should refrain from treating her like a child. The person sleeping upstairs is a grown-up now; keep that in mind.

❯ Depending on the laws of your state, your child is a tenant, with all the protections that the laws of your state offer. In other words, even if your adult child is not paying rent, you may not be able to just kick him out on a whim without an order from a housing court judge.

❯ Decide on the amount of rent your adult child needs to contribute each month. Draft a lease to map out how food purchases, housekeeping, communal and noncommunal areas of the home, guest policies, and rent will be handled, and establish a lease termination date.

Parents who want their adult children to leave the nest need to be clear about their expectations. When an adult child moves back home after a divorce, college graduation, or serving in the military, this is rarely by choice. Thus, in the initial days, after the awkwardness has dissipated, parents should hold a meeting to discuss their adult child's exit strategy.

■ Automatic Babysitter

If an adult child returns or never leaves home and has children of her own, the homestead parents need to clarify their own role. Often goodhearted grandparents are ushered into playing the role of automatic free babysitters. While grandparents have abiding love for their grandchildren, assuming they will take on the role of being frequent caretakers is discourteous. Grandparents should be specific as to their availability to babysit and whether they will charge hourly rates or late fees. Grandparents simply do not serve their adult children when they don't establish boundaries. This limit setting must happen because of the nature of their familial relationship.

■ Emergency Room

When I was notified of my father's death, never in my wildest dreams did I imagine the daunting efforts I would have to undergo to settle his estate. Like a frightening number of African Americans, my father died intestate—without a will. Therefore, it took months and several trips to the state where he resided to locate his legal papers and wrestle his possessions from two con artists who had stolen all of his money from his bank account. Suffice it to say that, after a lengthy hearing in which several financial vultures appeared out of the woodwork, a surrogate court judge appointed me to be executor of the estate. No child needs to experience what my brothers and I did.

Years earlier, my grandmother had simply written down her wishes on a sheet of notebook of paper and then left the paper with a trusted friend. Preparing your will is an urgent matter that you must take care of right away. Ignoring this obligation to your children could prevent the greatest transfer of financial stability to your descendants. Furthermore, processing a parent's death is an intensely difficult emotional period in the life of any child. Documenting your final wishes will prevent stirring up additional turmoil among your children and family members. Please take action: write a will today.

A National Center of Health Statistics study reports that blacks are about half as likely to have a living will, a will, or a trust as compared with the general population. Even more startling, according to the CDC's National Nursing Home Survey, blacks in home care and nursing homes are half as likely as whites to have a living will or other advance directives drawn up.

Not many parents are comfortable confronting their own mortality, especially with their children. However, too often in the black community, this conversation is had during the tumultuous time after a loved one has made his or her transition. The responsibility often falls to extended family members to attempt to determine the deceased parent's wishes as it relates to the rearing of children and the allocation of their possessions. Often the loved one's legal documents have been misplaced, and individuals step in to make choices that in life the deceased would never have approved of, especially with regard to his or her children. Create a family will for the sake of your children.

In addition to the distribution of your assets, a will also lists the people you would like to be the designated executors, trustees, and guardians of minors, along with other provisions that will assist in the fulfillment of your wishes. Some parents question the need for a will and instead prefer to rely upon the rules of intestacy succession to dispose of their estates. This is not a good idea. It cannot be overstated that parents need

Estate Planning Documents Every Parent Should Have

Living Will: A written document that allows a patient to give explicit instructions about medical treatment to be administered when the patient is terminally ill or permanently unconscious; also called an advance directive.

Trust: A legal arrangement in which an individual (the trustor) gives fiduciary control of property to a person or institution (the trustee) for the benefit of beneficiaries. Does not require filing in probate court.

Will: A document in which a person specifies the method to be applied in the management and distribution of his estate after his death. Requires filing in probate court.

not own wealthy estates. For example, if you want your family pet to be cared for in a certain manner, outline the specifics in writing. Depending on the state in which you reside, your children could be subjected to estate fees and court costs they may not be able to afford.

Preparing a will, living will, or trust is urgent for three key reasons:

1. If your wishes are not detailed, the state in which you live will decide for you how your estate will be distributed.
2. In the event of your passing, you need to make arrangements about who will raise your children (and how). Again, you would not want your surrogate court to make this important decision.
3. It is common that discord erupts among family members when settling the possessions of a loved one who dies intestate. Save your loved ones family conflict by being clear, in writing.

Consult with an estate planning attorney, because there are marked advantages and disadvantages, varying from state to state, between a will, a living will, and a trust. You should also be sure to review and regularly update your will, particularly after major life events such as the birth of a child, a death, a divorce, or a remarriage. Some people choose to review and update their wills on an annual basis.

Children have a natural curiosity about death, and as your family experiences the loss of family members, your child probably will ask you about the subject. Frankly, children are often more concerned about their own well-being than anything else. Again, depending on the child's age, your answers can vary in the detail you share. See the chart below for suggestions.

| Ages three to seven | Question: "My friend's mother died, and now she has to live with her grandma. Will you die too?" |
| | Answer: "Honey, not for a very long time. I love you very much and will make sure you are safe." |

Ages eight to twelve	Question: "What's a will?" Answer: "It is a piece of paper that states your wishes when you pass away."
Ages thirteen to seventeen	Question: "What will happen to me and my brother if you die?" Answer: "All of my legal documents (the trust, insurance policy, bank statements, and our attorney's contact information) are kept at our bank in a safe deposit box. They say who will take care of you. I also have scanned copies saved on my computer's hard drive."
Ages eighteen to twenty-five	Question: "Can I read your will?" Answer: "My will is a confidential document only to be reviewed when I pass away, but I have been fair in making certain that you will not have to absorb any court fees or estate taxes."

In addition to estate planning, parents need to organize copies of the following documents into one file:

- Birth certificates
- Social Security cards
- Passports
- Citizenship documents
- Copies of their driver's licenses
- Military discharge papers (DD Form 214)
- Marriage and/or divorce papers
- Copy of living will, signed and witnessed by an adult
- List of bank accounts with bank contact information
- Credit card numbers with bank contact information

- Title to your car(s), insurance documents, and registration
- Deed to your house, mortgage, and insurance documents
- Tax returns, W-2s
- Power of attorney paperwork
- Death certificates for any deceased family members

An attorney or trusted advisor (and depending on their age and maturity, your children) should know the location of your legal and financial documents. Life, infirmity, and death are inescapable. Without a doubt, these issues will affect your children and your descendants' quality of life. It is best to prepare before emergencies occur.

Closing Bell

"Money is only a tool. It will take you wherever you wish,
but it will not replace you as the driver." —AYN RAND

ON SEPTEMBER 17, 2011, a demonstration called Occupy Wall Street began in Zuccotti Park in New York City's Wall Street district. The protests attracted thousands of protestors, labor unions, and student groups, and then spread to cities throughout the United States and the world. Protestors rallied against economic and social injustice and what they considered to be the greed of banks and corporations. While the protestors captured the support of many African Americans, it is my hope is that parents and their children will "occupy" their personal finances. The ignorance and corruption occurring on Wall Street are a reflection of the habits of many of us who live on Main Street.

Once adult Americans, and parents specifically, become experts in managing their personal finances, this awareness will manifest itself on Wall Street. Gone will be the days when we refuse to discuss the influence money has in our lives and avoid taking the necessary actions to positively affect our families. Parents will educate their children about predatory businesses, subprime mortgages, and the importance of reviewing and understanding legal documents before signing them. Parents will educate their children about the pitfalls of prepaid debit cards and high-interest credit cards. Parents with "have" consciousnesses will begin to lead their children away from impulse spending and toward conscious saving and investing.

Fortunately, the power to change our country rests with our personal behaviors—the same behaviors our children imitate.

Now more than ever, we must build the knowledge and skills that will empower our children and us to live lives of prosperity, filled with respect for what healthy relationships with money can do. By instilling in their children healthy mindsets and an understanding of the language and behaviors that are intrinsic to the world of money, parents can rest assured that they will change the trajectories of their families for generations to come.

ACKNOWLEDGMENTS

DO I LOOK Like an ATM? would not be possible without the contributions of the parents who shared their heartbreaking and candid stories. These parents and their children represent a cross-section of the American story. People of all economic statuses, blue-collar and professional families, confided their secrets, many openly admitting their financial histories for the first time. And I thank each of them, those who needed to remain anonymous and those who did not. All of the names in the case studies in this book are pseudonyms.

My sincere appreciation goes to my agent and friend Sara Camilli for your loyal support, wisdom, and laughter. Though you represent many authors, I always feel as if I am the only one.

I profoundly appreciate each of the hundreds of youth who have attended the WorldofMoney.org Youth Financial Education Institute. You are the crown jewels of my life and the source of unending joy and inspiration. I love you all.

To the members of the WorldofMoney.org board of directors, financial presenters, the Parent Advisory Council, Leadership Council, and Community Artist Council, I thank you for your tireless efforts to empower our youth while creating sound financial legacies in your own families. I adore each and every one of you.

Thank you, Stephen Camilli, for your keen eye when I could see no more.

And to my editors, Jerome Pohlen and Kelly Wilson: Thank you for your humor and queries and your desire to support parents everywhere.

Special thanks and sincere appreciation go to Michelle Schoob, who volunteered to become a midwife in the birth of this book. Michelle's meticulous care has been a valued gift. And thanks to Ewurama Ewusi-Mensah, for your keen eyes and wisdom and understanding of nuance, and to Mary Kravenas and Josh Williams in marketing and publicity, for your efforts to spread the word.

Thanks to my dear brothers Paul and Jason for letting me hover. I love you both very much.

Last but not least, I thank the parents who, over the years, have entrusted the WorldofMoney.org Youth Financial Education Institute with your children's financial education. You have displayed the greatest love of all.

FINANCIAL WORDS EVERY YOUNG PERSON MUST KNOW AND UNDERSTAND

annual percentage rate (APR): The amount of interest a credit card holder will pay in a year in addition to his or her regular balance to use the credit card. There is no standard APR in the credit card industry. Thus the percentage can vary widely among different credit card issuers and even among individual accounts issued by the same company.

bank: A bank is a financial institution that accepts deposits from people and companies and uses these deposits to lend to other people and businesses at a high interest rate.

bankruptcy: A legal proceeding for a business or person who is unable to repay outstanding debts.

bond: Companies and governments will issue bonds in order to raise substantial amounts of funds; a purchaser of a bond may earn a return based upon accrued interest.

commodity: Commodities are generally resources that originate in the ground, such as crude oil, iron ore, gold, and silver, as well as agricultural products such as soybeans, rice, and wheat.

compound interest: Interest that is paid to an account holder by a financial institution on the deposited principal and also on any accrued interest.

consumer: One who buys products or services for personal use and not for manufacture or resale.

contract: A binding agreement between two or more parties for performing, or refraining from performing, some specified act(s) in exchange for lawful consideration.

credit bureau: An agency that collects and sells information about individuals' creditworthiness.

credit card: A card issued by banks that people and businesses use to purchase goods and services on credit and then repay along with a percentage (determined by the interest rate) of the money borrowed.

debt: An amount borrowed from a person or business with the express agreement to repay.

debit card: A card that allows a person to access only the funds available in his or her account, without paying interest.

deficit: The amount of money that an individual or government exceeds in their spending over their revenue.

dividend: A taxable payment distributed by a company to its shareholders from earnings.

diversification: A strategy to minimize risk in one's investment portfolio by spreading money among a variety of investments such as stocks, mutual funds, and real estate.

donation: Money or items given, not in exchange for financial or service reward.

FICO: Fair Isaac Corporation; uses analytical date to create credit scores for individuals.

financial media: Television, radio, print, or Internet broadcasts that report financial and business content.

501(c)(3): The Internal Revenue Service gives corporations or nonprofit organizations this designation to protect them from having to pay taxes; 501(c)(3) organizations are also known as tax-exempt organizations.

insurer: An individual or company that issues insurance products.

insurance: An insurance company replaces financial, medical, and property losses sustained by its customers.

interest: Interest is really a fee charged for borrowing money; it is a percentage charged on the principal amount, usually for a period of a year.

IRA: Individual retirement account; a tax-deferred earnings account that allows individuals to set aside monies until they reach age 59½.

Internal Revenue Service: Also known as the IRS; the federal agency that oversees the administration, assessment, and collection of individual and corporate taxes.

intestate: A person who dies without a will.

investor: An individual who commits money toward investment products with the expectation of financial return.

lease: A written agreement or contract whereby a property owner permits an individual or business to utilize property for a preestablished amount of time.

lien: A claim held against property to secure a loan or tax obligation.

money: Currency used for the exchange of goods and services.

mortgage: A loan used to purchase real estate.

mutual fund: A fund managed by an investment company that invests in a variety of assets on behalf of investors.

premium: Payment used to purchase insurance protection.

probate court: A court that decides issues regarding trusts, wills, estates, and intestate issues.

profit: Monies gained after subtracting expenses.

rent: Monthly payment made to a property owner, also known as a landlord, for use of a residence or commercial property for a pre-determined time.

retail: Sale of small quantities of goods or commodities directly to consumers.

Rule of 72: An approximate annual compounding rate required for money to double over a given number of years. For example, to determine the annual compounding rate required for money to double in eight years: 72 ÷ 9 = 8, or 8 percent.

tax: A mandatory payment ordered by a local, state, or federal government.

tax-deductible donation: Cash and property donations to qualified nonprofits, which are permitted to lower the donor's amount of assessed taxes.

trust: A trust acts in the same manner as a will but is not administered in probate court. Upon the death of an individual, designated executors automatically take possession of the assets.

wholesale: Purchases by businesses that intend to resell to consumers at retail price.

will: A will is a legal document, administered through probate court, that outlines the wishes of a deceased individual with regard to the transfer of his assets and management of his estate.

RECOMMENDED RESOURCES

▪ Books

Andrew, Douglas R., Emron D. Andrew, and Aaron R. Andrew. *Millionaire by Thirty: The Quickest Path to Early Financial Independence*. New York: Business Plus, 2008.

Clason, George. *The Richest Man in Babylon*. 1926. Reprint, New York: Signet, 2004.

Harper, Hill. *The Wealth Cure: Putting Money in Its Place*. New York: Gotham, 2011.

Hill, Napoleon. *Think and Grow Rich*. 1937. Reprint, New York: Tribeca Books, 2011.

Kiyosaki, Robert T., with Sharon L. Lechter. *Rich Dad, Poor Dad: What the Rich Teach Their Kids About Money That the Poor and Middle-Class Do Not!* 1997. Reprint, New York: Business Plus, 2000.

Lapin, Daniel. *Thou Shall Prosper: Ten Commandments for Making Money*. Hoboken, NJ: Wiley, 2010.

Stanley, Thomas J., and William D. Danko. *The Millionaire Next Door: The Surprising Secrets of America's Wealthy*. 1996. Reprint, New York: Pocket Books, 1998.

Tart, Nick, and Nick Scheidies. *What It Takes to Make More Money than Your Parents*. Vol. 1 of *50 Interviews: Young Entrepreneurs*. Denver, CO: Wise Media Group, 2010.

Timmons, Jacquette M. *Financial Intimacy: How to Create a Healthy Relationship with Your Money and Your Mate*. Chicago: Chicago Review Press, 2010.

Velshi, Ali, and Christine Romans. *How to Speak Money: The Language and Knowledge You Need to Know*. Hoboken, NJ: Wiley, 2011.

Writers of Wise Bread. *10,001 Ways to Live Large on a Small Budget*. New York: Skyhorse Publishing, 2009.

■ Websites

Allowance Manager: www.allowancemanager.com
    Helps parents and children manage allowances.
AnnualCreditReport.com: www.annualcreditreport.com
    The Federal Trade Commission provides free annual credit reports; other websites have lures to paid services.
Bankrate: www.bankrate.com
    Surveys approximately 4,800 financial institutions in all fifty states in order to provide objective and unbiased rate information to consumers.
BillShrink: www.billshrink.com
    Free cost-savings tool that works continuously to save you money on your everyday expenses.
Choose to Save: www.choosetosave.org
    Sponsored by the American Savings Council, this website provides financial education to adults.
Coupon Sherpa: www.couponsherpa.com
    Provides online shopping coupons.
FatWallet: www.fatwallet.com
    Online coupons and codes.
Federal Deposit Insurance Corporation: www.fdic.gov
    Insures bank deposits.
Feed the Pig: www.feedthepig.org
    Provides resources to save more and reduce debt.

4Chores: www.4chores.com
   A free online chore tracking tool.
Get Rich Slowly: www.getrichslowly.org/blog
   Offers cost-cutting tips.
Hands on Banking: www.handsonbanking.com
   Online interactive money program.
Internal Revenue Service: www.irs.gov
Investor Words: www.investorwords.com
   Investment and financial dictionary.
Jump$tart Coalition for Personal Financial Literacy's Reality Check:
   http://www.jumpstart.org/reality-check.html
   Your child may daydream about living on his own. This website
   shows your child how much it will cost them.
JuniorBiz: www.juniorbiz.com
   Money-making ideas for young people.
Khan Academy: www.khanacademy.com
   Provides free world-class education online.
LowerMyBills: www.lowermybills.com
   Free online service for consumers to compare low rates on monthly
   bills and reduce the cost of living.
Mint: www.mint.com
   Tracks all of your financial accounts in one place.
Money Talks: http://moneytalks4teens.ucdavis.edu/
   This interactive site teaches money management to teens in Eng-
   lish and Spanish.
myFICO: www.myfico.com
   Offers a free trial so that people can learn FICO scores.
MyMoney.gov: www.mymoney.gov
   Teaches basic financial education.
Savingforcollege.com: www.savingforcollege.com
   This "Internet guide to funding college" contains detailed informa-
   tion on various 529 plans.
SmartyPig: www.smartypig.com
   Free online saving tool for specific items.

Upromise: www.upromise.com
> An innovative company that helps people save for college through a rewards program.

Wise Bread: www.wisebread.com
> Offers cost-cutting ideas.

Compound Interest

Mind Your Finances: www.mindyourfinances.com
> Explains the power of compound interest and budgeting.

Moneychimp: www.moneychimp.com/calculator/compound_interest
_calculator.htm
> Online compound-interest calculator.

Financial Media

Black Enterprise: www.blackenterprise.com
> Premier business, investing, and wealth-building resource for African Americans.

CNBC: www.cnbc.com
> Cable news channel that provides interviews with business leaders and market updates.

Financial Times: www.ft.com
> International financial and business newspaper published in the United Kingdom.

Fox Business: www.foxbusinesss.com
> Cable news network that discusses financial news.

Wall Street Journal: www.wsj.com
> US-published international financial and business newspaper.

Investing

ShareBuilder: www.sharebuilder.com
> Online stock brokerage firm.

Philanthropy

YouthGive: www.youthgive.org

This organization helps to develop the next generation into compassionate givers and global citizens.

■ Organizations

WorldofMoney.org: www.worldofmoney.org
The Financial Clinic: www.thefinancialclinic.org

INDEX